# Invincible
# Thinking

BOOKS

IRH PRESS

New York

Library of Congress Cataloging-in-Publication Data

ISBN 13: 978-1-942125-25-9
ISBN 10: 1-942125-25-9

Printed in Canada

First Edition

Book Design: Jess Morphew

Cover image © Pobytov / DigitalVision Vectors / Getty Images
Interior Image © CkyBe / Shutterstock.com

# Invincible Thinking

An Essential Guide
for a Lifetime of Growth,
Success, and Triumph

# Ryuho Okawa

IRH PRESS

# Contents

CHAPTER ONE

# The Source
# of Invincibility

| 17 |

# Essential Lessons
# for a Life of Triumph

| 105 |

# Preface
## TO THE NEW EDITION

I published the first edition of this book in 1989 to offer keys to success in life using simple and easy-to-understand language. Since then, it has inspired and resonated with many readers—finding fans in every field, from politicians to corporate executives—and has sold more than two million copies in Japan alone. It has also been translated into foreign languages and has found its way into the hands of readers throughout the world. In the meantime, Happy Science, the organization I founded in 1986, has become the most influential religious organization in Japan and it is well on its way to becoming one of the major religions in the world.

I have decided to publish this new edition in light of the political and economic upheaval that the world has increasingly become embroiled in, causing many to feel uneasy about the future. It is my sincere wish to offer hope and courage to these people by proclaiming *Invincible Thinking*'s main message: we shall never be truly defeated in life.

Invincible thinking is a powerful attitude that enables us to triumph under any circumstance. It helps us learn from both successes and failures and grow into capable and exceptional leaders. Invincible thinking embraces the philosophy of positive thinking and the principle of self-reflection, which together help us shape our future as we face all the circumstances life brings. I present this book with an earnest hope that many of its readers will become outstanding leaders who will guide many others to the right path.

Finally, I would like to add that gaining thorough knowledge and wisdom about the ways of the world is an important part of enlightenment. When you read this book, you will clearly see that such wisdom is what distinguishes our organization from other so-called "cults."

*Ryuho Okawa*

FOUNDER AND CEO
Happy Science Group

# Preface

## TO THE ORIGINAL EDITION

Invincible thinking is an empowering attitude that gives us the power to truly triumph in life beyond superficial success. The ideas in this book are relevant to everyone, regardless of age, sex, or nationality. Whether you are young or old, a man or a woman, and no matter where you're from, when you read through this book, you will clearly see an infallible path to success opening up before you.

Life is like drilling a tunnel through a mountain. Everywhere we go, we may be hampered by floods or find rocks blocking our path. But these are the very times when we should use invincible thinking. Invincible thinking is a powerful drill that penetrates through the rock; it's the dynamite that opens a crack in the mountain of difficulties.

If you read, study, and savor this book entirely and thoroughly, making it your own, you will be able to boldly declare that you will never again know defeat in life, only triumph.

*Ryuho Okawa*

FOUNDER AND CEO
Happy Science Group

# THE SOURCE OF
# Invincibility

# THE THREE ESSENTIAL QUALITIES OF A LEADER

*Invincible thinking is* a mental attitude that gives you the power to turn any adversity to your advantage. With this mindset, you can bring about positive outcomes no matter what difficulties or hardships you may face in life. From this perspective, you will no longer see misfortunes and tragedies, but only a continuous series of opportunities for growth.

Invincible thinking is especially indispensable for those of us who will be the leaders of the coming era. We are constantly scanning our environment for indications of future directions and trends. At the same time, each of us is seeking what's truly valuable in life and wondering which path to take. A leader is someone who can see future trends, who can concisely and accurately guide those who are uncertain about how to make the best use of their abilities, time, and money, and who can show people what they need to do now. This is the mission of the truly awakened who will become the leaders of the coming age. So to become outstanding leaders, we need to be able to offer answers and guidance on the right direction in which to move forward. The purpose of this book is to show how to become such a leader. So I begin this book by discussing the three essential qualities of a leader.

The first essential attribute of a leader is to always be able to see into the future and stay one or two steps ahead of others. Those with foresight are held in high regard as outstanding and capable leaders. In the eyes of others, these people appear to be giants who can predict the future because of either their higher awareness or their prophetic ability. Gradually, people around them become drawn to their enigmatic personalities and follow them willingly.

However, the ability to see into the future alone is not sufficient to become an outstanding leader. Even if we can foretell what will happen, which may enable us to temporarily fill a leadership role, others will eventually leave us if all we predict are failures and defeats. So the second prerequisite to become a leader is to instill in others a feeling of hope for a bright future—hope that something good will happen if they follow our leadership. I believe this is the reason why my organization, Happy Science, has grown so much over the years. Many people have sensed that something good would happen if they joined this movement. No one would board a ship that they were afraid might sink. People decide to follow someone only if they can expect good things to happen as a result.

The third prerequisite for leadership is to achieve concrete results that will convince others of our leadership capability. These achievements do not necessarily have to be marked by a brilliant career record or awards for excellence. Whatever paths we take in life, the way we overcome the difficulties we face and the process we use to overcome them can be the proof that we have the qualities it takes to become an outstanding leader.

In looking at the lives of great figures in history, I've noticed that many of them came from unprivileged backgrounds. Even those who were born into privileged families often faced severe setbacks or adversities at some point in their lives. Whether they were born rich or poor, what inspired so many people were their endurance, resilience, and strength that enabled them to work diligently to overcome the difficult obstacles in their lives.

# 2

# ILLNESS:
# A TIME OF RECUPERATION
# AND SOUL SEARCHING

*You may wish for* a life that is always smooth sailing, in which everything goes exactly as you wish and nothing gets in the way of your happiness. As ideal as this sounds, it is actually the ups and downs of life that help us learn and grow. For example, we usually don't give serious thought to our physical condition when we are savoring healthy and vital living. But this doesn't mean that we should consider illness simply as the enemy of well-being and write it off as the source of misery and suffering in life, because we *can* actually find positive meaning in illness.

Let us consider why we become sick. If we look back and contemplate a series of events that may have led us to illness, we will see that there is always an early stage or a preliminary period before we develop an illness. This is when we see a sign that something is wrong with our physical body. We start to feel like we are coming down with something. We may feel pain, nausea, or other symptoms that prevent us from doing what we usually do. In a sense, this is nature's way of telling us to rest and recuperate when we are at the brink of collapse. If we were always healthy, we would take it for granted and keep working until we dropped.

So one positive role that illness plays in our lives is that it keeps us alive when we burn out. Illness forces us to temporarily stop working and rest so we can live out our life and fulfill our true purpose in this world. Illness can save and extend life by giving us time to recuperate. If we never fell ill, we might push ourselves beyond the limit and leave this world before our time. By forcing us to undergo a period of recuperation, physical ailments serve as precautions against life-threatening damage to our body.

This period of recuperation brings us a lot more benefits than just physical rest. When we become sick, we become introspective: we take the time to look within and reflect on our thoughts and feelings. We often neglect to look inward when we become busy with our social lives or preoccupied with external achievement.

We're at special risk when the goal of our life becomes getting ahead in a competitive society. That leaves us no room to care about anything else, and we start to adopt a falsely positive attitude and judge everything by outward results. In fact, many people today delude themselves into thinking that they are headed for success, unaware that they are actually living as a false self. Failures and setbacks, either at work or in health, await them at some point in life to serve as catalysts to help them find their true self.

# FACING SETBACKS ON THE PATH
# TO SELF-EXPANSION

*Adversity is a gift* from natural providence because it offers us an opportunity for inner reflection. And we are given this opportunity because periods of deep introspection are crucial for our soul growth. In fact, looking deep within and examining and delving into the inner self is an essential practice for becoming an outstanding leader.

To illustrate the type of person who is likely to face a setback that will force introspection and self-reflection, let us look at the life of a car salesman. This salesman is very successful at what he does; he sells cars one after another and gains new accounts and customers on a daily basis. Because he is so busy and preoccupied with taking care of his day-to-day tasks at work, he does not set aside time for his personal life, his family, and the people around him. He feels complacent as long as he can meet his sales quota of fifteen cars per month, and for the coming month, he's raising his target to eighteen cars sold. He is only interested in boosting his sales figures or meeting his quota and disregards the quality of the product itself, so he becomes oblivious to customers' bitter feelings of discontent about the product and service that he sells.

A good business in the truest sense brings lasting joy to the customers who purchase the product or service. But our salesman neglects the happiness and satisfaction of the customers who purchase cars from him. When things are going well, we often become too preoccupied with fulfilling our own desires and satisfaction to notice anything else, and we become inconsiderate of other people's feelings.

The salesman keeps achieving concrete results, boosts sales figures successively, and gets promoted to sales manager. He now has people working under him, which means he can no longer work at his own pace and is no longer evaluated only by his own achievements—as the sales manager, he is now responsible for the work of his staff as well.

He instructs his staff to do exactly what he does, which is meet their sales quota every month, no matter what, because he believes that that's what made him successful. The only instruction he gives his team is to sell certain numbers of cars, and he evaluates their performance based solely on whether they have achieved the target he sets. Because his only criterion for success is the achievement of the sales figure, he labels those who fail to achieve that goal as a burden to the company.

The sales manager feels frustrated that those working under him can only sell three to five cars when he can sell fifteen cars per month. A good manager would show them step by step how to sell more, but this sales manager gets impatient and starts to make the sales himself. He goes over the heads of his subordinates, directly contacting their clients and customers himself. The sales reps who work under him are naturally offended by their boss's actions and end up neglecting their jobs, feeling that if their manager feels so confident that he can do a better job, then he should handle it himself.

This manager may achieve his sales goal, but he is so keen on seeking his own success that he neglects to give serious thought to how the human mind works. He can't see himself objectively either, so he doesn't realize that the only reasons he is successful in sales are his audaciousness and impudence. He barges in on others and sells cars, believing that everyone likes him and is opening their hearts to him. He never notices that everyone heaves a sigh of relief as soon as he leaves. He has no idea that everyone is fed up with his presumptuous behavior, so he keeps pushing them, in the mistaken belief that he can be friends with everyone.

Needless to say, not all the sales reps he works with are aggressive like he is; some are cautious or sensitive. These people can't work in the same way that their bold and audacious manager works, so they develop different ways to make the most of their strengths and skills. They may engage in a new activity or learn a new hobby as a way to start a conversation with new clients, or they may increase face-to-face interactions with their customers as a way of promoting sales. But the aggressive sales manager finds this sort of approach very frustrating to watch.

Eventually, something will happen to force this arrogant and impatient sales manager to go through a period of self-reflection. He will be put in an adverse circumstance so that he can truly understand other people's suffering and sorrow. Setbacks and adversities will arrive to disenchant him from his belief that he is indispensable to the company and that nothing would get done without him.

It will come as a shock to him to discover that everything goes smoothly in his absence. His colleagues and staff may come to visit him in the hospital and try to comfort him by saying, "Everything is fine in the office, so please don't worry about work and concentrate on getting healthy." But these words are actually the most painful thing he could hear, because they make him feel as if he is not needed anymore. What he wants to hear is that everyone at the office is at a loss as to what to do without him. He wants them to beg him to return to work as soon as possible. This sort of experience shatters his reality. He is like a clown who suddenly realizes that his audience has left the theater while he's been immersing himself in his own performance under the spotlights.

If you find yourself in this kind of situation, you might feel disappointed to realize that your company can conduct business as usual without you, when you thought that you held an important position in the company. Sad to say, in reality, this is how the world works. Especially in the corporate world, there is always someone else who can fill your position as soon as you step aside. Even the CEO, who is often considered indispensable to the company, can be replaced. This is because the success of a business operation hinges not on the ability of one single individual but on the teamwork of many people. We should never forget the fact that we can fulfill our potential only with the help of many others.

# HARDSHIPS: INDISPENSABLE EXPERIENCES FOR SOUL GROWTH

*When capable people are* first starting out in their careers, they often devote themselves to proving their abilities. They do this because they crave recognition. They try harder and harder until they earn good evaluations. Strangely enough, however, the harder they try, the less they are appreciated. I'm sure many people have had a similar experience, and it can be quite difficult to figure out why this is the case.

This happens when our behavior is based on the mentality of taking love from others, which is the opposite of the mentality of giving love to others that I teach at Happy Science. When we try hard to win praise and admiration, those around us feel as if they lose out when they give the recognition that we crave.

If you look around you at work or at home, you will probably find someone who does things just to receive compliments.

But usually these are the people we are most reluctant to praise. Unable to receive recognition from others, they try even harder. But then, contrary to their wish, others start criticizing them for their boastful attitude and for showing off their capabilities. This is how they get caught in the dilemma: the harder they try, the fewer compliments they receive. They begin to complain that the world is an unfair place and blame others for not fairly assessing or acknowledging their ability.

What these people don't realize is that their obsession with receiving recognition and compliments prevents them from recognizing other people's abilities and strengths. They are only concerned about what will benefit them and have no interest in the happiness of those around them. They can only see others from the perspective of the support and help they can gain from them. As spiritual beings, others can sense that self-centered people like this will never bring them happiness, so they start to avoid them. They begin to criticize, harass, and even speak ill of those who crave recognition. This is how the situation gets worse and eventually backfires on them.

Trials and tribulations come into the lives of people like this as necessary experience for their spiritual growth. Hardships serve as indispensable experiences for the soul growth and so bring about not regression but development of their character. Setbacks and trials are not actually negative experiences, because they offer us the chance to polish our soul, better understand the feelings of others, and empathize with those who are going through difficult times.

So if you find yourself in the throes of a setback or adversity right now, I would like to ask you to look back at the way you have lived for the last several years or even the past few decades. Look within and ponder whether you have lived a well-balanced life. Consider whether you may have been preoccupied with your own achievement and neglected to appreciate what others have done. This deep introspection process is indispensable to our soul growth.

We encounter various situations in life that teach us important lessons, but the experience of overcoming difficulties and rising above adversity is essential for cultivating deep inner strength. When we triumph over hardship, we can turn it into a strength that shines from within, but if we give into adversity, we end up living with a negative image of ourselves as unable to conquer our difficulties.

Difficult times do not last forever. The lesson here is about how much we can learn from our difficulties and taking advantage of the opportunities they present. No matter how daunting the hardship you are currently facing may seem, learn all the lessons you possibly can from it.

# 5

# THE FOUR KEY ATTITUDES FOR OVERCOMING ADVERSITY IN LIFE

*When you fall ill*, suffer a crushing defeat, or fail miserably, you may despair and feel as if you are the only one who has ever faced such a miserable experience. But do not let difficulties or failures make you feel this way. Instead, open your eyes and look at the people around you with an open heart. If you look closely, you will realize that not all successful people have come this far without any failures or setbacks. You will find among them those who, despite facing difficulties and problems, continued to make the utmost effort to turn their adversities into springboards for success.

So think about those who have faced situations like the one you're facing now. If you're suffering from an illness, whether you're dealing with heart disease, cancer, or some other physical ailment, I'm sure you are not the only person in this entire world who has ever suffered from the disease. You will surely find someone else who has been afflicted with the same condition.

Franklin D. Roosevelt (1882–1945), despite having a disability that kept him bound to a wheelchair, carried out his duties when others in the same condition may have found it difficult to stay socially active. This shows that FDR chose not to live a life of excuses but did whatever he could do in the circumstances he was given. He made every effort to overcome his disability.

I have also heard a story of an American woman who lost her husband when she was still young, was rejected by her children, fell into poverty, and became seriously ill, but nevertheless rose to one of the highest positions in the U.S. government.

I'm sure those who have overcome adversities to reach great heights have learned lessons from their difficult experiences. I have discovered four attitudes that these people all share. First, they never bemoan their fate or blame others for their hardships. They are fully aware that doing so would do no good whatsoever. Never putting the blame on others nor despairing over their fate is the first attitude these people have in common.

The second characteristic they share is their acceptance of what fate brings them. Instead of mentally harboring "what ifs" and "if onlys," they embrace whatever comes their way, no matter how hard or cruel it may seem. They readily take it as their reality and consider how to go about overcoming it.

Their courage and determination are strong enough to accept misfortune as a reality of life.

The third attitude they share is an ability to always find lessons in adversity. They ask what the hardships they face are trying to teach them, and they keep searching for answers until they find them. The wisdom they acquire invariably becomes a priceless treasure that remains in their hearts for a long time.

The fourth mindset they have in common is self-reliance. They have no intention of depending completely on others or living off of others' help. They never let go of their independent, self-help spirit, even when they find themselves in the most disadvantageous positions. They walk the path they have been given on their own, never forgetting to make the effort necessary to help themselves. They accept their fate or whatever appears before them as it is, but they don't allow themselves to be complacent about it; instead they do whatever they can in their own right to break free from their adversity. All extra-ordinary people go through this process.

We may be tempted to wallow in self-pity, but this would prevent us from achieving greatness. Once we give in to the temptation to draw others' sympathy, we condemn ourselves to a life of self-pity.

You may suddenly find yourself in an unfortunate circumstance after years of building business success. Perhaps you fall ill or become disabled at the worst possible time. But as soon as you repine at your misfortune and start living off of others' help, your soul has given in to defeat. This is the very time you need to daringly accept your fate and commit yourself to overcoming it.

# 6

# OPENING UP A PATH
# WITH DETERMINATION AND
# PERSEVERANCE

*Overcoming the difficulties you* face in life doesn't have to be a momentous decision. You can open a new path by starting with a small effort you can make on your own. Ask yourself what you can do in the circumstance you are currently in. Even if you find yourself deprived of the gifts that helped you achieve success, you surely have other abilities you can use to move forward.

To discover your latent capabilities, look back on your life and ponder the skills or talents that your family, friends, or teachers complimented as you grew up. Perhaps you have some hidden aptitude that you have forgotten about. By tapping into your undeveloped abilities, you can open up new avenues for your future.

I once saw a documentary on TV about a man without arms who painted with his feet. He held a paintbrush between his toes and drew paintings that were of professional quality. I was very impressed with how he managed to not only paint, but also do just about everything using his feet.

This is a real-life example of someone who made great efforts to overcome difficulties. Many people would simply give up if they didn't have arms and rely on help from others for the rest of their lives. But the man featured in the show didn't let his disability take control of his life. Instead, he chose to take control of his life by using his feet to open his way on his own. He enjoyed art, so he decided to try painting himself, using his feet. He struggled at the beginning but got the hang of it little by little and kept improving his skills until eventually he became a proficient painter. His example shows that even if we were to lose our arms, we could still develop our feet to use as substitutes for hands.

If someone without arms could paint with his feet—using his toes to hold the brushes and squeeze out the paints—those without physical disabilities should be able to achieve anything if only they put their minds to it. Some make excuses about their inability to get ahead—they blame circumstances or say they lack talent—but if they really wanted to, they could study and obtain a license that would open the door to a new career or accumulate experiences in their area of interest to get one step closer to achieving their goals. The only thing they may be lacking is sufficient effort or the willpower to keep trying.

In fact, we have already received a great deal, including perhaps a healthy body and an education that our parents may have provided support for. With the gifts we've been given, absolutely nothing should stand in the way of our achieving whatever we set our mind to.

When we consider the severe hardships that people with disabilities have overcome, the accumulated efforts they've made to reach their goal seem all the more fascinating. Those who didn't quit, despite adverse circumstances, awaken us to our possibilities as the ones exuding so much potential and energy. This realization is to do all we can do—much more than we do now—so we can give love to as many people as we can. The more privileged we are, the greater our contributions to the world should be. Becoming aware of our potential to serve and help many is of utmost importance.

# 7

# OVERCOMING OUR LIMITS WITH INGENUITY AND INNOVATION

*I, myself, am always* wishing to work harder and contribute to the happiness of as many people as possible. Still, there are times when I feel bounded by my physical limits. This is when I turn to invincible thinking; instead of using my physical power, I use my thinking power to overcome my limitations. I constantly think of innovative and creative ways to get things done. Ingenuity, invention, and discovery are vital elements of invincible thinking.

In fact, the development of our organization, Happy Science, was made possible by a series of creative and inventive ideas that we implemented. Whenever we run into a brick wall or a bottleneck, I make it a rule to carefully consider the next step the organization should take, instead of merely bringing greater zeal to doing the same things in the same way. So, if we find that our physical limitations are preventing us from achieving our goals, we should accept the fact that there are limits to what we can do physically but at the same time come up with creative ways to overcome our physical limitations.

The first approach you can take when you come up against your limits is to consider if there's any part of your job that you can delegate to others. Ask yourself what someone else can do for you that you don't have to do yourself. Another approach may be to train others so they can take over some of your tasks. Receiving assistance and support from others often facilitates the overall development of the organization.

A good example of someone who used invincible thinking is Konosuke Matsushita (1894–1989), the Japanese entrepreneur who founded Panasonic. His frail health prevented him from running his business by himself, so he had no alternative but to entrust some of the work to others. In 1933, he set up the world's first divisional system, which was a new structure that consisted of a parent company and subsidiaries.

Today, a divisional organization structure, which divides a company into a number of semi-autonomous divisions that focus on specific product lines, is quite common and has been adopted throughout the world. Delegating responsibility to the manager of each division allows large corporations to run their operations smoothly.

In a top-down management system, in which the head of the organization makes all the decisions, the entire business reaches its limit when the leader reaches his or her capability limits, and that prevents the organization from expanding and developing its true potential. The divisional system allows the leader to achieve greater results than what he or she could achieve alone, because by assigning managers of each division the role of company president, the organization functions like a conglomerate of companies.

Matsushita turned his disadvantage of not being able to run everything on his own into an advantage to expand his business. He saw his limits as opportunities for others' growth. He realized that if one person was responsible for everything, others would not be able to develop their potential. Matsushita completely trusted in others' capabilities and gave them full responsibility for running their part of the business.

For example, when Matsushita opened a new branch in Kyushu, some three hundred miles from the head office in Osaka, he knew he couldn't personally go there to manage the new office. He sent in a young man and completely entrusted him with the new office. Matsushita told the young manager that Matsushita couldn't take the train down from Osaka to supervise him, so he would have to carry out business by himself. He believed that this system would enable his employees to exert their full potential to achieve great success.

He had learned through his experience that people would develop into efficient and capable workers if he believed in their potential and completely entrusted them with the job.

And just as Matsushita expected, his business developed into a multinational electronics corporation with a workforce of a few hundred thousand people.

Matsushita's example shows that we should not let our own limitations restrict the development of the whole. In most cases, when we feel we have reached our limit, it's not our lack of ability but a lack of ideas that makes us feel that way. We can overcome our limitations by coming up with creative and innovative ideas.

Sometimes, everything goes exactly the way you want it to, but good times don't last forever. When things turn sour, instead of carrying on in the same old way, take a moment and ponder if there are any other ways of doing things, any ways of getting around the situation.

# 8

# RECEIVING HELP AND SUPPORT FROM OTHERS

*As long as we* try to do everything all by ourselves, we will inevitably reach our limit. So to expand the scope of our work, we will eventually need the help of others. A good idea can be brought to fruition only with the support of others.

Suppose you are a fish peddler. If you feel content doing just this, you will probably spend your whole life selling fish on the street. But if you decide that you want to do more than that and expand your business, you might start exploring how you can get more people to come and buy from you. Through experimentation and observation, you might notice that quite a number of customers come to buy fish every time you go to a certain area between four and five o'clock in the evening. Let's say you can sell five times more fish in an hour than if you went to a different part of town. Once you become aware of the sales potential of this particular place at a certain time, you will naturally go there to sell fish every day between those hours.

You might also consider whether there is a demand at any other time of day and find that many people wish they could buy fish at a later time near their house when they've forgotten to buy it at the grocery store. You can meet their demand if you can find a suitable location to set up a stall in their neighborhood.

By discovering potential demand at a particular time of day at a particular time, you can make considerably more sales more effectively than by randomly driving around town to find customers. The profits you earn by doing this may allow you to hire an assistant who can help you sell more fish during the same hours. Even if you attract twice as many customers as before, you will lose them if you can't serve them. With two people selling fish, however, you can double your efficiency; for instance, you might be able to concentrate on selling the fish while your assistant can be the cashier.

As your sales increase, you can employ even more people and buy more stalls to sell even more fish. If you can expand your business until you own perhaps five stalls, you'll be able to buy good quality fish in bulk at lower prices. Let's say you purchased twenty to thirty mackerels a day when you started your business with a single stall. An increasing number of successful stalls would allow you to buy one hundred, two hundred, or even five hundred mackerels. This could work to your advantage, allowing you to haggle at the market and purchase them at a lower price, which, in turn, can enable you to sell them at a lower price, increasing your customers' satisfaction.

Business growth usually accompanies an increase in the number of employees and improvement in the quality of service, which produces more satisfied customers who can now purchase better quality goods and services at a better price. This creates a virtuous cycle in which things can only get better. Corporations that grow rapidly over a period of twenty to thirty years, from a small mom-and-pop business to a major corporation with thousands of employees, are usually successful in creating this virtuous cycle.

The essential key to creating this virtuous cycle is to become aware of the potential of the business. If we remain oblivious to the numerous possibilities, we could go on in the same old rut for thirty or forty years. But if, as the example of the fish peddler shows, we pay attention to and become aware of where and when it would be best to do our business, from the perspective of better serving our customers' needs, we can create a virtuous cycle of business growth.

Whether you can explore and discover the potential of your business and innovate based on your discoveries is the watershed that determines the future growth of your business. Eighty to ninety percent of business expansion is hampered by the limits of the owner's abilities. It is often their desire to maintain the status quo that prevents their business from developing.

Whether it is a coffee shop, a sandwich bar, or a hamburger stand, those that develop into nationwide chains have unlocked the secret of using ingenuity to achieve more than what a single individual can do alone. This is the secret to expanding a business.

What I am trying to say here is this: when you feel stuck and cannot seem to find a way forward in life, it could simply be that you're trying to do everything all by yourself. But there is a limit to what one person can accomplish singlehandedly. If you really want to achieve great things, you will definitely need other people's help and support. You will need to win over many people.

# 9

# TWO SECRETS
# FOR ACHIEVING SUCCESS

---

## Finding a Demand

---

*There are two* essential secrets to succeeding in business.

The first secret is to always anticipate people's needs and make sure their demands are on your radar. Businesses start with a market need. Businesses that have achieved rapid growth have all begun with someone who sensed and noticed a demand.

Where there is a demand, there always is a business opportunity. If your business remains unprofitable despite many years of hard work, it is probably because there is insufficient demand for your product or service. The same is true if you're running an educational institution. A continuing shortage of students may mean that you are not providing the classes they want.

One good example of this is how the traditional Japanese sweet bean pancake evolved to meet people's needs. This Japanese pancake traditionally had only one type of filling, but today features various types of fillings, from custard to chocolate. The cake shop that first started selling these various types of Japanese pancakes made considerable profits. The original Japanese sweet bean pancake was only popular among the elderly and small children, but when the shop replaced the filling with custard and chocolate, the pancake became a hit among young women, which led to increased sales. This example shows that business success depends on meeting the needs of many people.

The same holds true for any other business and even for homemakers. If you are a homemaker, your job may not produce tangible profits, but you will find opportunities for success if you can discover your family's needs. Finding a demand is the first secret to success.

## Planning for Growth

The second secret is to use the original demand as leverage to find the seeds of further growth. In other words, always think of how you can keep developing your business. When you make observations from this perspective, you will be surprised to discover many possibilities for your business.

To take the previous example of the Japanese pancake shop, the owners stopped innovating after their initial success. They became content with their success and stopped trying to come up with new products, which limited the business's further development. If we succeed in one area, we should not let it confine us. Instead, we need to keep tapping into our business's potential by using the initial success as a springboard to achieve greater success. This is how we can continue advancing.

# 10

# IMPROVING OUR FINANCIAL SITUATION

*Many people feel frequently* troubled by mental or emotional distress. As a matter of fact, 70 to 80 percent of mental and emotional problems can be solved by financial means. You may not believe me when I say this, but I can assure you that you can resolve 80 percent of the issues that are causing you distress right now if your income increases tenfold.

Let's say you feel tired all the time. The reason for this could be as simple as your long commute from your suburban home to your office in the city. It takes long hours to get to work every day, because you live far away from your office. Let us now think about how you can solve this problem. One solution may be to rent a house near your office. Another solution could be to hire someone to drive you to and from work. Looking at it this way, the issue of constant fatigue and frustration can be solved with money—money you can use to rent a house close to your office or to pay for a chauffeur.

Another common issue people struggle with may be the difficulty of taking care of a sick family member at home. This problem could also be solved quite simply by hiring someone to help look after the family member. Even a child's poor performance at school can be solved if the parents have the money to hire a tutor or pay tuition for a top preparatory school. The parents may be pressuring their children to work harder to do better at school, but they may simply not be receiving the level of education they need to reach their academic potential.

In fact, the root cause of the family problems and issues we struggle with today is often financial. And finding the solution starts with considering different ways to improve your financial situation. Suppose your career seems to have come to a standstill and you expect only a small increase in your salary for the rest of your life. You can either be content with what you will earn or think out a plan to increase your income in some other way.

Perhaps you can find some way of earning a secondary income. Developing your expertise in your field of interest may lead to a salary increase. You may discover a hidden talent for writing and find that the book you've written in your spare time has the potential to sell and become a source of extra income.

We don't necessarily know what will lead us to prosperity. And that's why we need to keep thinking and seeking a new path to the future. We are often bound by limits of our own making, so it is extremely important to think outside the box to find our way forward and to improve our situation. Don't get discouraged or feel frustrated by the difficulties and hardships you're going through. Instead, embrace adversity as a springboard to progress and future success.

# 11

# DISCOVERING
# THE INVINCIBLE SELF

*Take a moment and* contemplate the possibility that you are the one limiting your potential and capabilities. Are you letting past failures take over your life? Do you have a fixed image of who you are or what kind of person you should be? You will become the person you think you are, so you need to remove your self-imposed limitations and keep believing in the person you want to become. "You are what you think" is an eternal truth. As I have often said, our thoughts are very powerful. So to create our future, we should tap into our willpower much more than we do now.

This topic of willpower reminds me of an issue that many people in Japan struggle with today, which is a lack of educational achievements or background. These people are haunted by not having gotten into a prestigious school or received a higher education decades ago. By binding themselves to this past, they are actually labeling themselves as failures and letting others treat them that way.

But if they looked around, they would find any number of people who achieved great success even with little formal education. I don't think these people thought that their educational background would hinder their ability to achieve success. I know of a financial vice president who works at one of the top trading firms in Japan. His formal education only went through ninth grade, but he holds one of the most important positions in his company. I'm sure he made two or three times more effort than others to make up for his lack of education, but he didn't let his educational background get in the way of achieving success.

Some people suffer from an inferiority complex because they weren't able to keep up with their studies in college. But if you think about it, we spend an average of four years in college, and there's a limit to how much one can study in four years. So even if you couldn't complete all your studies in four years, if you continue studying for ten more years, I'm sure you will be able to master what others learned in four years. Even if you don't feel confident that ten years is enough, twenty years would surely be sufficient to cover all the material that college students learn to earn an undergraduate degree. Whatever your field of study is, if you put in three times as much time as others did, you should be able to learn everything they learned.

An inferiority complex related to a lack of education or intellectual ability is quite common these days. But if you justify your current situation by a lack of education, that may be the very reason you are treated unfavorably. The problem is often that our minds are stuck in the past: past failures remain strong in our thoughts.

What really matters are the efforts you have made since finishing your formal education. What path have you taken, and what have you achieved that you can feel confident about? We can always compensate for a lack of education by investing our time and effort in diligent study. So it is our lack of effort and strong willpower that we should regret. We should all work hard to make up for any adverse factors that we believe have affected our lives.

We all feel inferior to others in some way or other, but we shouldn't let our inferiority complexes define who we are or take over our lives. We can overcome our inferiority complexes only though our own endeavors. I strongly believe this, and I hope that you will not run away from your past failures and mistakes but instead face them squarely.

My suggestion for those who feel frustrated by a poor intellectual foundation is to start studying a wide range of topics and subjects to broaden your perspective. This is the most effective remedy for this type of inferiority complex.

I say this because one common characteristic of people who didn't receive a higher education is difficulty thinking in general terms or seeing the big picture. This is because they often get a specialized job that requires technical skills or expertise specific to that field of work. In many cases, their knowledge and experiences are limited to the field of their specialty. Without an opportunity to receive higher levels of education before specializing in one area, it is difficult to see things from a wide perspective. Broad knowledge is an essential foundation for developing our potential.

People can change greatly over the course of a decade or two, but many people are unaware of this. Even those who graduated from a top school cannot always maintain their level of knowledge if they stop studying, whereas those without a diploma can become more knowledgeable if they continue studying. No one seems to keep track of the intellectual effort people make after leaving school.

But in fact, the qualification exams held at Happy Science serve as a good measure of our members' intellectual endeavors. These exams test understanding of the different levels of teachings of the Truths, and the results do not necessarily reflect the participants' academic backgrounds. This shows that academic records do not necessarily measure intelligence or spiritual awareness.

I ask you not to let your own negative self-image limit your possibilities for future growth. I truly believe that we become what we think we are. If you can develop a firm belief in this truth and integrate it into your life today by making concrete efforts on a day-to-day basis and progress as steadily as you would climb a ladder, one step at a time, I guarantee that you will see a path opening up before you and that you will discover an invincible self that keeps triumphing no matter what happens.

Chapter Two

THE KEYS TO TURNING

# Your Perspective
# Around

# 1

# CHANGING
# YOUR PERCEPTION

*A common dilemma we* face in life arises when the values we most cherish conflict with each other. We all have been through the anguish of being torn between two opposing choices, wishing we could avoid making a decision so we wouldn't have to suffer the hardship of giving up either of them. Some of my readers will recognize that this dilemma has been at the root of their present distresses.

Whether large or small, life's dilemmas often involve making a decision between taking the path on the right or the path on the left, to move forward or retreat backward. But in some situations, we can't reach the best decisions by looking for a simple "yes or no," "right or wrong," or "this or that" verdict, because either path we choose may lead us to one undesirable consequence or another. This is how our problems often lead us into a pit of frustration and despair.

But by taking an altogether different perspective on the situation, we open up possibilities for unique solutions we haven't thought of or considered before.

In this chapter, I would like to explore how, when we come up against a problem or adversity with no ideal resolution in sight, turning our perspective around can lead to a creative, constructive, positive solution that lets us fulfill a future of success and happiness.

This mindset is a little different from the capacity to distinguish right from wrong and choose one without considering other alternatives. Rather, it is based on the belief that every problem—whether in our relationships with others or in the circumstances that surround us—holds positive, constructive solutions.

Religious views can strongly influence our perceptions, dualism being one traditional principle that's given us a way to make sense of and find order in the world. For thousands of years, the idea that the world is a dichotomy between good and evil has been a foundation in religious discussions of individual life and conduct. In this view, the world is a duality of right against wrong: the pure heart against the wicked heart, the right intention versus the wrong intention, and virtuous conduct in contrast to vicious conduct. This perspective has helped us distinguish virtue from sin and identify which ways of living will lead us to heaven and which will lead us to hell.

But at the same time, it has cultivated a habit of dualistic thinking. It makes it feel natural to try to sort everything around us—every person, event, and circumstance we come across—into one side or the other. We may even feel ill at ease until we've managed to label everything in our lives as good or evil.

When we see the world only in this way, we risk allowing positive possibilities to escape us and foiling our wholehearted intentions to live well.

Imagine an alien from outer space who comes to Earth and lands his spaceship in Japan just as the monsoon season is coming into full force. As he sets foot on our planet, his very first experience of it is days on end of torrential rain.

His initial impression will be that Earth is a decidedly drab planet. If he never considers what discoveries he might make if he were to cross over the horizon, he might get back on his spaceship and go back to outer space without ever having experienced all of Earth's true marvels, diverse cultures, and natural beauty.

While many parts of Earth receive rain, we find other weather patterns everywhere we go. Even wet climates enjoy plentiful sunshine during their dry seasons, or sometimes even in the same day as a rainstorm. This foreign being from another planet could simply stay put and wait patiently for time to pass; he wouldn't have to stay longer than a month at most to see the clouds parting and the world graced with sparkling sunshine. Patience is all he needs to discover that Earth, in fact, offers a comfortable habitat.

What lies in store for this being's journey of exploration hinges on his capacity to perceive that Earth may have more positive qualities than what meets the eye. If he determines the value of this planet based solely on his first negative impression, he will be forsaking its true potential and will have to drift through space for several more decades in search of another planet. That is a choice of needless hardship that he would be imposing on himself only for the lack of a bit of patience.

In the same way, we humans often, as a result of a simple misconception, needlessly meet trouble halfway. Do you feel you wouldn't be so unhappy right now if only you had chosen a different partner? As many as 80 to 90 percent of married couples experience these feelings about their partner. Their conscience may tell them that it's not right to perceive their marriage that way, yet they can't hold back from wondering how their life might have turned out differently if they could have predicted the future and had the chance to find someone else while they were still young. Or they might think about separating from their partner so they could be with someone new. Perhaps some of my readers have spent thirty or more years thinking about their partner this way.

What can we do in situations like this? What should we do when we find ourselves in circumstances that feel less than ideal? First, we can change our beliefs and perceptions. There may be helpful new perspectives that we have never thought of before, and we can discover these perspectives with persistence. Second, we can use our ingenuity to come up with creative solutions to resolve the dilemmas we face.

# 2

# FINDING NEW POSSIBILITIES AND SOLUTIONS

*Let's imagine that your* spiritual life is a precious aspect of your happiness and well-being. You are looking forward to attending a seminar this weekend by a highly acclaimed spiritual speaker, and you expect this seminar to foster your spiritual, emotional, and mental growth, as well as your connection with your spiritual community. But your spouse is against your going out for long hours while he or she is spending time at home. By going, you are sure you'll be disappointing your spouse and likely fostering an argument, but by not going, you are certain you'll regret missing this opportunity. You are torn between two aspects of life that you cherish, and you don't know how to make the right choice.

As much as we wish it weren't like this, life presents us with any number of these predicaments. When we run into them, we can let them drive us into grief and anguish—or we can believe that there has to be an alternative solution. We need not choose between only two options; instead, with per-sistence, we can resolve them by searching for creative solutions that lead to the ideal outcome we wish for. Perhaps we'll conceive of a way to make the two options work in harmony, or maybe we'll be inspired with some other kind of ingenious idea.

In this situation, you could explore ways of fulfilling both of your desires, for instance, by taking your spouse with you to the seminar. Or you may think of another completely different and constructive solution.

However we try to solve our dilemmas, by thinking creative-ly and tapping our ingenuity, we're certain to find a positive solution to any predicament that arises in life.

Turning your perspective around is quite simple. You do not need to have achieved a certain degree of consciousness to be able to change your perception. Everyone holds the potential to do this, whatever their purpose or role in society may be. Let's explore how I found a unique solution to a conflict I once faced in my career. By shifting my perspective, I was able to continue pursuing two important missions in my life.

The dilemma I faced was that I was pursuing a career as a spiritual author while, simultaneously, I was seeing a rise in my opportunities to deliver lectures to large audiences. As a basic principle, those who write books for a living are bound to confront periods of stagnation in their productivity when out-side engagements become more frequent, since these engagements eat into their writing time. This is why authors so often seek to escape and be in solitude, whether in a serene lodge in a wooded retreat or by traveling. It's impossible to produce a work of writing without minimizing human interaction.

I was certainly not an exception to this rule. I frequently had to consider where to spend my blocks of time; I often had to ask myself, "Am I to choose writing, or should it be speaking?" But as I looked hard at my predicament, an insight told me to consider whether these two careers were truly in conflict. When I opened my mind to the perception that there could be a way for them to work together somehow, the solution came to me.

What was the idea that allowed me to balance both aspects of my career so I no longer had to sacrifice either of them? This book in your hand was the very product of my search for a solution. This book, in fact, was put together from a series of four lectures on the power of invincible thinking.

By using my lectures as a basis of the chapters in this book, I developed a way for both my jobs to work in harmony. This wholly eliminated the need to divide my time between writing and speaking. I decided to give eighty-minute lectures, then transcribe them on paper, and finally combine them into a unified book. This idea meant that I no longer had to spend time in seclusion to write my books.

This solution may not be ideal for every writer. For example, some writers find that their spoken words don't sound pulled together enough when put in writing. Since our spoken language usually sounds different from our written language, their lectures often don't appeal to their writing aesthetic, and that makes them unwilling to publish their lectures as they are. Unless they feel open to being less fastidious about their writing and are willing to be freer in their selection of words and sentences, they won't feel comfortable publishing their lectures.

This plan worked for me, however, and that is because I chose from the very start to release my perceptions about how standard writing should sound. I determined from the beginning that speaking style would be my signature writing style. When we consider what readers want to get out of a book, we realize that they're not looking for a perfectly crafted work of writing. Rather, they're looking for valuable content that's worth their time to read and learn.

For this purpose, what is most crucial for an author's style is that it allows readers to grasp the ideas and read through the work with ease. This means that whether a book is based on a lecture transcript or not, proper training and practice can help us create a book of good quality. Any doubts that other authors may have about this method stem from their unwillingness to let go of their preconceived perceptions about style. But by consciously letting go of their limiting beliefs, they will open up the possibility of making both of their careers work in unison and will not have to resign them-selves to giving either of them up.

Of course, for this method to work out, I needed to work my ingenuity even further. For my idea to succeed, I had to weave enough content into each lecture to give it the substance it needed to serve as a book chapter, and I only had sixty to ninety minutes in each lecture to accomplish this.

What was the key that enabled me to develop my lectures to this degree? Over the years, I've used a particular practice to train my mind to absorb what I learn and put forth my ideas. It's been my practice to underline the key sentences I find on each page of literature I read, and by doing so, I commit them to my memory. The rest of the book leaves my memory, so I'm left with just the essence of each work I read. Whether I'll remember the title of every book is another story. But I've trained my mind this way to keep freely accessible at my fingertips the ideas that I most value—those that my mind has absorbed and made my own. The years of cultivation to make my mind work this way have proved to be of great benefit in developing my lectures.

When you've trained your mind to operate this way, it also becomes second nature to know which parts of your lectures will be the parts your readers will want to highlight and re-member. This proved to become a useful skill for me, because the key to creating a satisfying chapter with depth is to incorporate at least two to three such lines into each page. And if I succeeded in developing my lectures to this degree, then each chapter would have enough substance to satisfy my readers. It was as simple as that. This was a skill that I was able to cultivate through practice, effort, and willingness.

This was how I turned my perspective around to solve my work dilemma. Anyone can do this, no matter what kind of work they do. Each time we practice it, we improve our ability to invent new ideas, and it becomes an ingrained habit. The key is to accumulate effort upon effort in cultivating your mind this way. Over time, this capacity will gain strength and fuel your competency in life and at work.

When we practice this skill and make it one of our strengths, we find that we're able to quickly perceive the heart of our problems, identify the conflict, and devise creative ways to bring them into harmony. There are times, of course, when the first idea doesn't work, in which case we'll quickly conceive of another one, and then another, all in just a matter of moments. Solutions arise so smoothly, erasing all traces of any problems or distress, making way for only hope to fill our mind. With each new solution we conceive, we're giving birth to new hope—our first hope, our second hope, our third hope, and on until we've transformed each of our problems into hopes for the future.

# 3

# THE POWER OF
# REVERSE THINKING

*Turning our perspective around* can be a solution for enhancing our productivity at work.

Everyone, at some point in life, is likely to experience the feeling of getting stuck in a work rut and confronting a substantial decline in productivity at work. These are the times when workers resign themselves to feeling satisfied as long as they're logging in long hours at the workplace. Despite this, they can't escape the gnawing feeling of being chased by deadlines. Often, these are people who have been working for ages without taking a single day of vacation because they're reluctant to burden others and they're afraid of all the work that might accumulate in their absence.

For some, this situation may escalate into a pattern of self-punishment. As they insist they can't possibly find the time for a vacation, they encourage others to take time off of work before them, only to find additional work falling on themselves.

They are the ones who end up filling in for others while they're gone. As a result, their productivity suffers even further.

You might know someone who has gotten stuck in this pattern of negative thinking, or you may recognize that you suffer from this mindset yourself. Workers who find themselves in this predicament are suffering from a low-spirited mindset that keeps them from taking vacations.

When you find yourself in this predicament, open your mind to the possibility of taking a vacation anyway. Even if your workplace doesn't let you take more than three days off without being subject to the wrath and criticism of superiors and associates, don't allow it to stop you. Carry on, and consider taking not just three days of vacation but an entire week. Try thinking through what will happen if you do this.

The first thing that comes to mind will perhaps be fear of the hole you'll create at the workplace by being away from your daily tasks. You may fear that you'll not only cause your superior's and associates' work to stall, but also burden your clients, customers, and business partners.

You may also worry that your vacation would invite shaming and judgment from your superiors and associates. This is, in fact, the most common reason many people choose not to take a vacation. Many people feel self-conscious and fear that taking time off would make others perceive them as lazy, frivolous, and inconsiderate. It's no surprise that surveys are finding that many workers these days are settling for fewer days off and not taking full advantage of the vacation days that their workplaces offer.

We've now identified the obstacles to your vacation. In the face of such obstacles, instead of giving in to defeat, you can practice reverse thinking. You can shift your thinking to look for ways to make your vacation possible. The key is to find a way to get your much-needed vacation while leaving not a single burden behind and gaining a positive growing experience for your soul. Reverse thinking is a way of transforming roadblocks into driving forces you can use to help you achieve your goal and gain something beyond your goal in the process. You'll discover that, contrary to your preconceived beliefs, there surely are ways to attain your goal if you put your mind to it.

For example, let us imagine that you want to take a vacation in a month from now. To achieve this goal, you can begin by devising a plan to complete the work you'll need to have finished by then in advance. Plan to put the hustle into your work so that you'll have accomplished so much that nothing will remain for you to do when your vacation comes around. When someone comes to you, you want to be able to say, "Work? I don't have any. I've finished everything that was on my plate for the next six months."

With effort, you can achieve this goal. Prepare to spend the next month or so putting in the highest level of productivity you possibly can. Because not only do you want to take care of the work that's due a month from now ahead of time; you also want to do the same for the subsequent month—that way, you'll be able to evade the critical eyes that'll fall upon you on your return.

As you go about this, you will find that a lot of your work overload has been more imaginary than real. You may have unconsciously set aside some of your work out of a fear of having nothing left to do. You feared going to work one day and finding nothing to keep you busy, so you've been planning ahead to spread your work out evenly over the course of the next couple of months.

You can easily take care of this kind of work ahead of time if you put your mind to it. Here, you can use your fear of feeling guilty and becoming the target of shaming to your advantage: you can make these fears your springboard. Allow these feelings to spur an intense drive and devotion to your goal. By doing so, when your first day of vacation rolls around, you may realize that you've finished not just six months' worth of work, but a much greater amount—maybe even nine months' worth. With that much of your work accomplished, you will be leaving for your vacation with the utmost peace of mind.

You can also take advantage of your fear of burdening others: think of this fear as an opportunity to clarify the work you do. You are familiar with the way you handle the work that comes to you each day, but your coworkers are not. In order for them to fill in for you as seamlessly as possible while you're away, they will need to know how your work should be dealt with and managed in your absence.

If they receive a call for you, need to handle an administrative matter for you, or need to meet with one of your clients, how can you make sure they're prepared to handle these situations the way you'd like them to? A manual is very useful for this purpose, because it can show them exactly what they need to do in each situation. If your manual makes it clear to anyone who reads it just what needs to be done, then your colleagues will be able to take care of these tasks for you. The key is to clearly outline your instructions: What issues may arise, and how should they be resolved? What kinds of questions will your colleagues be asked, and how should they answer them? By preparing your coworkers for the specific types of situations they may run into during your absence, you can completely resolve your concern.

By contrast, if you leave them in the dark without a prepared manual or a single word of explanation, it would make sense for them to be angry. If they receive a call from your client asking for a response from you by the end of the day, for example, they need to know how to respond. Going away without preparing them for this kind of situation will no doubt invite unnecessary ill-feelings and criticisms. In that case, you'd have no one to blame for the problem but yourself.

We have explored two ways to turn a negative situation or predicament at work into an opportunity to increase our productivity and competency in one fell swoop. While we all have our own unique walk of life, everyone can practice this way of thinking and accomplish similar goals.

For instance, a shop owner can also practice the power of reverse thinking. Because of the nature of the job, a shopkeeper may feel that she's serving customers all day long and that her days fly by in a haze. But if she stops and considers, she may realize that certain hours of the day are actually not as busy and that her business's peak hours come in waves. So while she believed that she was working continuously for twelve hours each day, reversing this thought will allow her to discover that her business does offer a few slow hours that she can use for a different activity or purpose.

In a similar way, some restaurant workers may insist that they need to work all day. But if we examine their restaurant more closely, we'll find that its busiest hours are between 11:00 AM and 2:00 PM for lunch, and then they have a lot of time until the next busiest time of day begins at 5:00 PM. Restaurant workers who feel they're being chased by the clock all the time and struggle to find time outside of work may be able to use at least two of these hours for themselves, if they consider how to manage their time more productively.

They may not have taken this time for themselves before because they were using it to prepare for the evening hours, which always require tremendous work. But what if they used their time in the morning for this preparation work? If you ask, they might tell you that they have only thought of using their mornings to prepare for lunch. The idea of also using morning hours to prepare for dinner service has never occurred to them, because they've been following preconceived notions that this is the way they work and following the same grind day in and day out. By taking care of preparations for both lunch and dinner during the morning hours, they may be able to free up some time for a break after lunch.

Similar cases can be found in abundance and can be solved by making this same kind of shift in thinking. I hope that many readers will make use of and benefit from the power of reverse thinking. When you allow your mind to open to the full array of positive possibilities, you can solve these kinds of problems and dilemmas one after another.

# 4

# A TREASURE TROVE
# OF INNER WISDOM

*If we liken our* rate of success in life to a baseball player's batting average, then our goal is to raise the "batting average" of our life. The best way to do this is to always be searching for new perceptions and solutions. Adopting this mindset can make a world of difference in the degree of success we achieve in life, compared to the outcome we may invite if we adhere to a black-or-white perspective in making decisions.

I believe that this mindset in itself can give us at least a .300 batting average, by analogy. It's difficult to measure success in life in percentages. But if our present success rate is below .500—let's say .300 or .400, both of which lie on the side of defeat—we may be able to raise our score by an additional .300. That change alone can boost us over to the side of success.

While this wouldn't raise our success rate to a perfect score, no amount of effort that we put into looking for positive perspectives and solutions will be in vain. At the least, each attempt we make to find new possibilities will help us in the next dilemma that we face on our journey of life. Of course, there will be times when we suffer defeat no matter how much we persevere. However, the possibilities that we conceive, comb through, and lay out in our mind will remain with us and will eventually come to fruition down the line when the need for them arises—whether in one, two, or five years from now.

Put another way, turning our perspective around is a mindset of determination to use every failure or setback as a springboard. It is about believing that there can be nothing in this world that doesn't have a positive use. In Japan, there was a time when the whaling industry provided vital resources of food and oil and each whale was treated with such respect and appreciation that not an ounce of skin, flesh, or bone was ever put to waste. Likewise, we can find a positive use for every failure, experience, event, and circumstance we ever face in life.

The same attitude holds true for the people we cross paths with. We enjoy being in the company of amiable people who inspire happy feelings within us. On the other hand, there are people we abhor spending time with, and these people become our teachers in life. We can learn many life lessons from them about human character and how certain aspects of a person can imbue others with adverse feelings. They offer us a wealth of learning materials that we can study closely to gain a deeper understanding of what gives rise to an unpleasant personality, continuous cycles of defeat, abrasive speech, and a tendency toward pessimism. They bring us a valuable opportunity to gain important wisdom about the human heart.

The answers we gain from meeting our difficulties with an attitude of learning from them become preserved in a treasury of our own. As spiritual beings, the savings we put into the bank accounts of this world are not the only type of savings we reserve through the course of our life. Through the people and experiences we cross paths with, we learn the reasons behind the things we see happening around us at a deeper level of consciousness. These precious experiences of inner knowing are jewels of gold that stay in the eternal treasure trove of our mind. We can freely draw on these reserves of wisdom whenever we want. The truly successful are those who have great reserves in their treasure trove of wisdom.

# 5

# FINDING GOD'S PURPOSE
# IN EVERYTHING

*I would like to add* a crucial point to my discussion of turning our perspective around to find the positive element in any circumstance: the aim is to practice not only on ourselves, but also on the world outside us. Changing our perceptions may seem similar to ideas from secular-style theories of self-realization, but they are not exactly the same. Changing our perceptions is not just about self-growth and personal achievement, and it's not about making our journey through life smooth sailing.

Changing our perspective to see the positive light in everything is founded on a core idea that has a deeper purpose. The foundation of this attitude is the belief that God did not create this world and all of creation in vain.

As earth-bound human beings living in this world, we sometimes give way to negative emotions such as resentment, dissatisfaction, and covetous desires, and this world may sometimes appear to us as the most terrible place to live in, full of vicious people. The foundational premise of changing our perspective is to believe that the opposite of this must be the truth—that there can be no such thing as a vile world inhabited by vile people. Adopting this positive view of our world is the crucial element to shifting our perspective.

The universe and the world we live in now were brought into existence by God and designed with divine benevolence and purpose. God wished for this world to become a world of splendor exuding such divine qualities as goodness, beauty, and purity. These were the qualities He drew on to will this world into being. Without them, he would not have intended for this world to exist at all. It's true, indeed, that problems abound and what seems to be evil exists. But this was not God's original desire.

If you believe in some form of spirituality, you are likely to have accepted some conception of the universe as not a creation of coincidence, but a creation of sacred intention, and you likely believe that such a profound design must belong to an existence of the highest consciousness. Have you ever wondered, then, why you continue to suffer inner pain and feelings of discontent despite this benevolent intent?

It may be because your heart still lacks the full conviction that this world was born of divine purpose. Perhaps you still have hesitations, confusions, or misconceptions that keep you from believing that this world was spawned from God's goodwill and imbued with positive purpose.

Pondering these questions will lead you to the shift in perspective that you hope to find. You'll be guided to an inner realization that, deep within, there remained a part of you that passed judgment on others and the world we live in, or perhaps a part of you that passed judgment on your own fate in life. Imposing verdicts of right and wrong based mostly on whether things disadvantaged you or not, you perceived the advantages to be small and the disadvantages to be great. So this world looked as though it was filled by utter darkness, as if it were a hell-like existence. But if you cast your thoughts back to the beginning of creation, when God imbued this world with splendid purpose, you'll see that you were mistaken in your beliefs and conceptions. You'll gain an inner knowing that your view of the people and this world as wrong and vile was mistaken and that to change your fate, you will need to begin by changing your beliefs and perceptions.

If you are convinced deep within that this is God's world of goodness and splendor, then your surroundings should not appear vile to you. They appeared vile to you because you harbored misconceived perceptions that you then saw projected onto the external world. Just as the whale was a valuable resource that nourished the lives of many people in many ways, everything we find in this world is a precious material that can promote our spiritual growth and enrich our souls. Going through life with this perspective will help us to never allow any precious resource for spiritual learning and nourishment to go to waste.

# 6

# FACING LIFE'S ORDEALS
# WITH A POSITIVE MINDSET

*In the previous section,* I talked about a premise that underlies shifting perception: the belief that this world we live in was created by God. This leads to the second premise: the belief that, as spiritual beings, we undergo eternal cycles of reincarnation to foster our spiritual growth. The concept of reincarnation, the idea that we go through eternal cycles of life, death, and rebirth, is closely related to the well-known concept of karma.

When we see the purpose of our lives in this world from a spiritual perspective, we see that all our experiences foster our growth, and everything in our world begins to look different, even adversities and hardships.

The ordeals that give us the greatest grief and despair are our most valuable learning opportunities, laid out for us much like the problems in a workbook. They reveal the unique purpose that this present life is intended to serve for our souls. They give us empowering knowledge about the true, most positive meaning of our existence.

When you are faced with an ordeal, at first you may feel trapped in a pit of despair with no hope of escape. But when you consider your life through a spiritual lens, you will be led to recognize that you are really standing in the midst of what could be the most meaningful problem in the workbook of your life. This could be a most pivotal juncture of your spiritual training in this world. This could be the most exciting, exhilarating time of your life.

The ordeal you are now contending with is the title match you have been training for during the previous month, two months, or even six months. You've come to the point of no turning back—the point at which your only choice is to step into the ring to face your contender squarely. You have endured brutal training while dreaming of this day and shadowboxing against an invisible foe. Now the opportunity has come to put your training to use in your most important match, the one for which you were born.

When this moment arrives and the referee has called for you, your match is about to begin, and no time is to be wasted. This is not the time to escape into a bathroom break! It's the time to step into the ring and rise to the moment.

From a spiritual point of view, your preparations truly began a much longer time ago, decades, centuries, or even millennia before the day you were born into this world. You invested a great deal of time in this preparation while you were in heaven, until your heart felt ready and fully resolved to meet your true challenge in this world. With this much hope and expectation on your shoulders, there's no room for hesitation or excuses. The task that's laid before you is as clear as day: your mission in the ring is to bravely face your opponent and take him down.

In reality, of course, there is no physical opponent to contend with and so no reason to fear bodily injury. Instead, you have the obstacles of life to combat. But even these obstacles, which appear so vividly real to us, are no more than a kind of mirage or illusion in reality. They are projections of your karma that borrow the shape of the problem or ordeal that you see. So the obstacle is never our external environment, but rather the karmic inclinations within our own mind. The true foe we must deal with is the karmic tendency of our soul.

I have just explained what it means to turn our perspective around to a different point of view, to show you how this shift works to ignite our passion and zeal in the face of obstacles. Picture, right now, the many years you have spent preparing to face the most important ordeal of your life. Now how does it feel to be standing in the ring right this moment? I think that you will feel the burning determination that lies within you.

But if, instead, you hear your thoughts say such things as, "I was never the brightest crayon in the box," "If only I hadn't grown up in such disadvantaged circumstances," "It's because of my parents," "My brothers are to blame," or "We were always struggling financially," what will this do to your determination? Your determination will most likely fail you.

This is what would happen to a professional boxer's morale if he were to come out of the red corner, touch gloves, and begin to say to his opponent, "I didn't train as much as I should have for this match. And besides, my legs feel like weights, they keep wobbling, my back's been under a lot of pain since yesterday, and my shoulders have gotten swollen. Not only that, I have weak muscular build, lack mental grit, and hired a bad coach who never trains me. But I guess it doesn't matter, because it doesn't make a difference to me whether I win or lose. In fact, what's the use? Everyone expects me to lose anyway." With this negative attitude, it's not hard to guess that this boxer's fate could only be utter defeat.

We don't show up to a title match baring all our weaknesses in this way. This is not the attitude we want to bring to any important fight or competition, if we intend to win it. No matter how many disadvantages we have, our foes should never hear or find out about them from us.

Whatever our advantages or disadvantages, we need to put on a brave face and persist with a positive mindset. If you're a boxer of 140 pounds and have a lighter build, then choose to stand proud and tall, imagining that you are 160 pounds instead. Better yet, envision yourself twenty pounds heavier than your opponent, and let him feel the intense pressure of your much "larger" stature. These are the ways we can shift our perspective toward the bright side of life's many ordeals.

# 7

# OVERTHROWING A NEGATIVE SELF-IMAGE

*Insecurities about our* physical imperfections are a common cause of negative thinking. It's a dilemma so universal that probably very few people, if any, would admit to having absolute confidence in their looks.

I don't think we could find anyone, anywhere in the world, who truly embodies the flawless, ideal image of perfection; everyone has something they want to fix or change about how they look, no matter how perfect they appear in other people's eyes. It is said that even Marilyn Monroe felt discouraged by her short stature. Physical flaws are a natural part of being human, so it doesn't serve us to allow negative thinking to perpetuate the struggle with a negative self-image.

If you suffer from feelings of inferiority or a lack of self-confidence, I recommend doing this simple exercise to help you see yourself in a positive light. Try to think of every aspect of yourself that you feel unhappy about, whether physical, mental, or spiritual, and write them down. When you're finished listing them, look at this list of flaws and weaknesses and count out how many you've come up with.

There might be at least a few on your list, but it's very unlikely that you found more than twenty or thirty of them. If anyone finds one hundred or as many as two hundred attributes to feel unconfident about, I would be genuinely impressed, and perhaps that would make them a type of an "inferiority genius." If you ever want to give this a try, see if you can find one hundred physical flaws, and another one hundred mental and spiritual weaknesses. It will be quite an impressive feat if you succeed in finding this many.

As you go through your list, ponder the question, "Is this really a flaw? A weakness? A fault?" For example, a lack of sensual appeal is something that many women might write down as a weakness. But is this really a negative quality? If we pondered this thought, we'd realize that it might not be a disadvantage after all. Women with strong sensual appeal may feel that other men are attracted more by their physical qualities and less by who they really are as a person, causing them to feel less appreciated for their inner beauty than they'd wish to be. If we look on the bright side, a lack of sensual appeal might mean that we're more likely to find a soul mate who loves and appreciates us for who we are within.

Many of our self-criticisms arise from our subjective notion of ourselves and are not objectively true. By simply reevaluating our self-perceptions, we can often see our negative qualities in a positive light. When we do, we'll feel positive and confident about ourselves and ultimately gain the courage to improve and become a better version of ourselves.

# 8

# CONQUERING LACK OF INTELLIGENCE

*It's also common for* those who lack confidence in their intelligence or level of education to suffer from a negative self-image and feelings of futility and worthlessness. These feelings often lead to a lack of motivation to improve and stifle our potential to change and grow. This is why, when we believe that these feelings represent the truth—that we truly are worthless—we leave hardly any possibility for our intelligence to grow.

If you feel this way about yourself but would like to change, you can conquer your negative frame of mind by looking at the bright side of your lack of intelligence. Even though sometimes it's necessary to be aware of where you stand, the realization that you are not as smart as others can become a positive force that you can use to kindle your zeal for self-improvement and inspire you to persevere tenaciously toward it. And that's not all: your lack of intelligence means that your life offers an infinite supply of knowledge just waiting to be gained, making this life your joy, delight, and thrill.

Imagine what your life would be like, in comparison, if you were a fast learner who could read a hundred books in a breeze and still recall what was inside them. Some exceptionally intelligent people are capable of this kind of feat. But it's somewhat of a shame to think how quickly their pleasure comes to an end.

Perhaps your pace of reading is much slower than this—maybe it would take you ten years to read that many books. But that is an endeavor that is worthy of admiration and offers positive blessings. With the large number of new books that come out each year, being a slow reader means that you will always have additional titles from which to learn and to add to your reading list. With books constantly accumulating on your list and an increasing amount of knowledge to be gained, you'll have no choice but to find a way to elongate your lifespan to have enough time to read them all.

Since I've authored more than 2,200 books to date and expect many more to come out each year, my readers may not be able to catch up with them until after I have passed from this world. So, for example, if your goal is to read all the books I've published before your life comes to an end, then you will have to live much longer than me to accomplish this goal.

By casting a positive light on your lack of intelligence in this way, you find a constructive goal that will allow you to spend your life aspiring toward self-growth and longevity—a plan far more worthwhile than resigning yourself to being stifled by a lack of confidence and to living a shorter life than you might have.

If you are in your later middle age, a period when you're approaching retirement, you may feel as though it's too late to set such a goal. But I recommend that everyone in their fifties and sixties spend time considering how they truly want to spend the evening chapter of their lives. Most people who've reached this point have thought about how they'll want to live for the next five to ten years but have probably not considered a longer time frame than that. Most assume that they'll probably only live into their sixties or seventies and figure that if that's all that remains of their lives, it's not worthwhile to give much thought to the future.

If you've reached this point in your life and this is how you've envisioned your future I urge you: dare to dream to live much longer. My advice is for everyone to think positively about their journey through aging and to expect to live up to the ripe age of 120.

Now is the time when you should begin putting a plan in place to determine what you will do during this imminent chapter of your life. For example, if you're currently sixty years old, you now have sixty more years to live. Six decades of life belong to you now, and you'll need to draw up a plan for them. These years are too precious to be spent aimlessly, even if you spent the first half of your life without a clear goal.

With this many decades to plan for, it's as if your current age is that of a toddler. Then in ten years' time you'll reach the stage of adolescence, followed by the period of early adulthood. This may mean that by your real age of ninety, you may have an opportunity to fall in love again. Carry on in this way until you finish your life planning. If you're one of my readers, you may hope that this will give you enough time in your life to read many of my books and put them into practice before you move on to the next world.

Even if your life carries you to the age of ninety, and that is as far as it takes you, what of all your hopes and perseverance will there be to regret? Your plans and aspirations will never be in vain and will never go to waste. I hope that many readers who feel that they lack intelligence or are facing the approach of elderly age will think positively and be inspired by it to live with hope and purpose, always aiming toward self-growth and longevity.

# 9

# LIVING WITH PURPOSE TO EXTEND OUR LIVES IN THIS WORLD

*With the power of* a positive mindset, we have the ability to elongate our lifespan. With effort, we can exercise our power to change how long we'll live in this world, regardless of what statistics say about our average life expectancy.

Life is made of many seasons, and these seasons are marked by periods of transition and great change that we plan for ahead of time. For example, some of the transition points that commonly arrive in the later stages of life appear at the ages of fifty-five, seventy, seventy-five, or eighty.

But while these major turning points can be expected, they are not absolute. Like a weather forecast, they serve as a prediction to help people prepare for what weather is in store in the near future, but at the same time, human predictions can be wrong; most weather forecasts are based on probabilities of 80 percent, 60 percent, or 50 percent. This means that, in times of transition and change, when a new chapter of life is about to open or when our life is about to close, we can still change our life's direction. The key is to change the way we think about how we want to spend the remainder of our lives.

Put another way, we need to know the reason we want to extend our time in this world. We need to have a purpose. Unless we do, we'll have no choice but to depart from this world. But if our desire is to stay, we simply need to create a reason for our continued presence.

So the secret to elongating our life is to find a purpose we wish to serve, an aim we want to work toward. Since the most common reason for our existence in this world is the work we do, it is important to look to the possibilities that lie in the senior chapter of our lives and create a plan for the work we would like to fulfill.

I plan to eventually offer more teachings for those past their youth, but as I said earlier, we should basically begin with the aim to live to the age of 120. Because when we look at life from a long-term perspective, we see that most of our short-term or imminent worries and problems will ultimately resolve themselves and vanish, and that understanding will help us see clearly what we need to do from that point on. Then we can work toward accomplishing each goal we set for ourselves, one by one, while still keeping our minds open to the possibility that our lives may come to an end earlier than we've planned.

In contrast, those who are presently in their young

adulthood have many years ahead of them to plan for. To decide how they'll want to use the one hundred years of life that are still ahead of them, they'll need to find more than just one objective. They have the opportunity to serve multiple goals in their lifetimes.

Just as a fireworks show is far more spectacular when two, three, or four varieties are combined into a medley, preparing a variety of goals and purposes to work toward also makes life more beautiful and worthwhile. Young people may also want to add a rocket or two or a delicate sparkler into the mix.

So my advice for those who are currently in the chapter of young adulthood is to begin now to sow the seeds of many goals that you wish to blossom when each new chapter of life arrives—for example, at the ages of thirty, forty, fifty, sixty, and so on.

Doing this will broaden your character and cultivate your mind. Planning out a long-term life plan is essential, because cultivation isn't a speedy process. We cultivate our soul not only by fulfilling our purpose right now but by feeding it the knowledge and experience that we gain over time. The knowledge and experience we gain as we pursue our interests may or may not seem useful straightaway, but it invariably serves us and nourishes our soul regardless.

Whether or not the seeds you cultivate have the chance to blossom into this world, you have nothing to lose by planting and cultivating them. When your life comes to an end, you will take with you only what is inside you. So whether or not your efforts have left their footprint in this world, it is still a valuable use of your time to grow the things that hold the most worth for your soul.

I hope that the keys to turning your perspective around that I have presented in this chapter will help many people find the positive purpose in their struggles, conquer negative thinking, and live a life of purpose and light.

Chapter Three

ESSENTIAL LESSONS
For a Life of
Triumph

# PRACTICAL SOLUTIONS TO CAST LIGHT ON LIFE'S BASIC CHALLENGES

*When life challenges us* to overcome adversity and misfortune, we may wish for more than overarching theories of success to guide us. In moments like this, we are often desperate for clear measures to take to resolve our problems. Many who picked up this book likely did so seeking concrete principles that would illuminate the solutions to their present hardship. They hoped that this book would clear up most of their worries and distresses and help them move forward through life with a positive mindset.

For this reason, in this chapter, I would like to offer lessons about the most basic life issues that we need to learn from and overcome in order to keep triumphing throughout our lives. The principles that I present will help you cultivate a balanced mind-body relationship, build financial abundance, find an ideal spouse and people who will change your destiny, and create a spiritual legacy.

My advice speaks to concrete, commonplace aspects of our lives, but it also holds the power to guide people to happiness and salvation, and this is why I wanted to give these topics a place among my principles of the spiritual Truths. Their every-day nature does not make them less valuable or to be shunned. My aim is not to provide spiritual teachings solely on a high plane of awareness; I also want to offer lessons that empower people to gain their own salvation and happiness. I think that it's only in achieving this aim that I can confidently say that my teachings illuminate the world with guiding light.

In the following sections, I cover these themes one by one to help you master the bare essentials of conquering these issues as you go through life. While the topics I discuss here don't represent all aspects of invincible thinking, they do represent its most fundamental facets. I hope that these principles offer some vital pillars of inner strength that we can all use to blossom bouquets of our own experience and wisdom, for our ability to flourish from them is very important to our lives.

2

# FOUR LESSONS FOR CULTIVATING MIND-BODY BALANCE

## Imbalances in the Body Can Foster Imbalances in the Mind

*The first key to* a life of triumph is to correct the imbalances in your physical health. I have often said that we are spiritual beings, not just physical bodies. But we currently live in this physical world, and our physical bodies are our principal means of self-expression. In this sense, no one is exempt from the physical principles of this world, not even someone whose soul was of sacred stature in a previous life. When such a soul is born again into this world, it cannot appear to others or express its thoughts purely as divine, formless energy of light. It needs to take on a physical body and communicate its wisdom physically, as others do, in the words they speak, the expression in their eyes, or the thoughts they put down in writing.

My spiritual philosophy is not a denial of the physical body, nor is it meant to devalue the physical body's role in life. My previous books have discussed many spiritual themes, including the problems that arise from within our minds as well as much larger-scale themes related to the will of the grand Universal Consciousness. In the end, though, the underlying purpose of each of my books always comes back to the impact of these things on each individual's soul. And when we think about how we should live in this physical world, the relationship between the mind and body is clearly a vital aspect we need to consider.

In particular, when we want to look within our minds to address the problems we face, we cannot ignore the need to resolve the negative spiritual influences that all of us have to contend with while we live in this world. Practicing self-reflection works very effectively on these problems, but sometimes the first step is to address any underlying imbalances we might find in our physical well-being, since our minds and bodies are inextricably connected and both work within the boundaries of physical principles. To live in this world, we all need to learn to manage our physical health to protect our minds from imbalances in our physical bodies, and we must always put in the work to continuously maintain a state of physical well-being and vitality.

## Navigating Your Body through Imbalances Is Key to Managing Your Health

Our physical bodies are like bicycles; they will stay in good condition as long as we learn how to ride them properly and maintain balance using the appropriate care. Can you remember when you were first learning to ride a bicycle? Perhaps you were half skeptical, at first, that a thin, two-wheeled vehicle could hold you up, remain balanced, and be maneuvered around. Compared to your safe, child-sized bicycle that was equipped with trusty training wheels, the adult version must have looked very unstable and dangerous to ride. You probably thought, "How do you sit on top of two wheels and manage to keep them balanced, all while you're peddling, moving forward, and making stops and turns as you go? What happens when you have to ride uphill or downhill? Will I be able to make it to the top? Will the brake be able to stop me when I'm going downhill?"

In spite of our initial anxiety, however, we spent time practicing riding our bicycles every day and eventually learned to balance them as masterfully as if they were extensions of our bodies. The physical body is very similar. It is like a vehicle that in the beginning feels like a prison to our freedom and impossible to tame. But through the steady steps we take to learn how to control them, our physical bodies grow to become intrinsic parts of who we are.

Our physical bodies become very useful when we learn how to balance and maneuver them. But they can pose problems for us if we start to lose our control. Losing balance of the physical body is like a child trying to ride an adult's bicycle or one with failing brakes or broken handlebars. These issues will make your bicycle—your body—very dangerous to ride.

Being constantly mindful of the condition of your body and correcting imbalances when they arise is without doubt the first step toward victory in life—and with effort, we can expertly manage our bodies' well-being on our own. It's like how we periodically inspect our bicycles' tires to make sure they're properly inflated and check to make sure our handlebars and brakes are in good working order.

It's not a good idea at all to be negligent and ignore these problems. If you don't refill your flat tire with air or you forget to repair your brakes, they may not work when you need them the most. If a car speeds past in front of you all of a sudden and your brakes and handles are broken, you could get hurt very badly, all because of a negligence that you could have avoided. It's the same with our physical body. It's vital for our safety and lasting well-being that we stay aware of our physical condition and restore balance when it's off.

## You Are Solely Responsible for Cultivating Your Physical Well-Being

To maintain balance, it's vital that we feel responsible for the well-being of our physical body. Our physical bodies were designed to be vital and healthy as long as they're nourished and cared for through health-conscious and self-aware living. So, if a problem arises with our health, we only have our own carelessness to blame. No one but ourselves can give our bodies the mindful attention and care they need to stay balanced and vibrant.

It's important to think of maintaining the balance of our physical bodies as one of the basic tasks in each of our workbooks of life. Someone I know who used to be in the Japanese Self-Defense Force once told me how they conduct parachuting training. They practice their jumping beginning at lower altitudes. They start at fifty feet off the ground and then move on to a height of 250 feet, atop a tall tower. And finally, they train by jumping from an actual airplane flying at altitudes of seven hundred to a thousand feet to practice opening their parachutes at the proper distance from the ground.

In every training session, the soldiers maintained their own parachutes. Since any case of equipment failure could cost the soldier's life, it was the rule for each soldier to be responsible for looking after their own parachute. After all, there would be no time to complain to anyone else about equipment problems during a free-fall through midair.

This may sound like a bad joke, but it's an important perspective that also applies to our responsibility to love and take care of our own body. As the parachute is to the soldier, our physical body is to us. A parachute's failure to open or any damage that it might suffer would pose a tragedy for the soldier, just as an impairment or injury to our physical body—whether planned for or not while we were in the other world—would pose an ordeal for our soul's spiritual training in this world. The responsibility is always ours to make sure that our body is not put in harm's way.

When we suffer damage to our physical bodies, our minds can become affected as a consequence. When this happens, we need to take the responsibility of addressing our minds as well as our bodies. If we neglect to take care of our health, our bodies will become vulnerable to illness, and no one is exempt from this universal rule. Like a tire that will become flat if it's punctured by a nail, the physical condition of the body will decline if it doesn't receive proper rest, nourishment, and compassionate care.

We can also compare the body to a professional baseball player. If he were instructed to be the opening pitcher in every game for an entire year, it's unlikely that his arm would last more than a year before giving out and becoming unusable, no matter how robustly he were to train in preparation for the season. This is why it's often said that pitchers should rest their arms for at least four days between games.

It's easier to understand the importance of maintaining the body's balance when we think about a professional athlete. But it's harder for it to sink in when we're talking about our own bodies.

We need to tune into the wisdom of our bodies to understand the level of strain they can endure, how much rest we need to give them to restore their energy, and what methods of fitness and maintenance will allow them to unleash their full potential. It's very difficult to know the answers to these things. No one else knows the answer, not even our teachers at school.

Just as we are the only ones who can take care of our minds, we also need to manage the health of our bodies—even if we have the support of our family to help us in some ways. It's important that we realize that no one else will be able to guide us in this respect, and it's up to our own self-discipline to treat our physical problems and restore our bodies to balance.

# Nurturing a Balanced Body Cultivates a Resilient, Healthy Mind

You may know people around you who have grown more susceptible to complaining as they've aged into their sixties, seventies, and beyond. Their distress is usually accompanied by increased anxiety and worry about their future. We may think that this is a mental issue, and that may be true to some extent. But at the same time, increasing complaints can also be an outcome of the physical decline they are experiencing due to aging.

As people grow older, their bodies begin to show signs of aging. It often begins with a weakening in their legs that causes them to be less active and mobile. This greatly restricts their freedom, and as their frustration builds due to their physical limitations, they begin to feel more agitated with the people around them and become susceptible to complaining about them. The complaining hurts the people around them, giving rise to disharmony in the home.

The root of this problem, which may seem to arise from the mind, is very simple: their lack of exercise during their retirement is creating imbalances in their minds. This, in turn, affects the whole family and causes a lot of division and heartache in their relationships with their friends and loved ones.

But if we understand the source of the issue, we see how simple it is to prevent it by restoring our bodies' balance. If we get exercise when we commute to work, then once we retire, we can make an effort to incorporate more exercise into our day-to-day routines. If we work at home, we can find ourselves declining physically as a result of either overeating or being undernourished because of excessive dieting. In this case, the root cause is a lack of moderation and balanced self-control.

For example, one of the kinds of overeating we often see is a craving for sweets and other sugary foods. Some people love eating snacks like cookies, cupcakes, and ice cream so much that they restrict their intake of other foods just so they can satisfy their sugar cravings. They may or may not realize that by depriving their bodies of nutritious foods, they are destroying their health.

While I sympathize with their love of sweet foods, our bodies cannot cope with such extreme treatment; they cannot be nourished properly solely from sugar. Our bodies need nutritious, whole foods to fuel and maintain all their functions properly. If our internal organs begin to fail as a result of poor diet, we only have ourselves to blame.

The same can be said about those who develop cavities from eating too many chocolate bars and too much candy. We can't ask God to be responsible for our tooth problems; we have to take responsibility for ourselves.

Living with the mindset that we are fully responsible for managing the balance of our bodies is vital to our lives and to our mental well-being. Exercise, especially, is an area of life that no one else can take the initiative to help you with.

I can't emphasize enough that exercise and the maintenance of our physical well-being is an essential must for our overall happiness in life and our ability to get through tough times. We should consider our health a precious investment that requires consistent care, and we should adapt our exercise and other methods of self-care to our unique circumstances and practice them within the reasonable scope of our capabilities.

Imbalances in the body give rise to imbalances in the mind, whereas a vital and healthy body fosters a vital and healthy spirit. The effort we put into our physical well-being will ultimately be rewarded by a strong sense of mental well-being.

In the same vein, I also recommend that, when something doesn't feel right with your physical condition, you practice introspection to find the cause of your body's imbalance—and on days when your body feels strong and healthy, practice positive thinking. A euphoric state of mind and favorable times tend not to promote the introspective state of mind you need for self-reflection. When you're feeling down, on the other hand, it's easier to reflect and make discoveries about what you might need to improve. By aligning your practice of positive thinking and self-reflection with shifts in your physical condition, you'll be able to better manage the well-being of your mind. I hope that this advice will help you maintain a balanced and vibrant body and mind to support you through life's joys and challenges.

# 3

# FOUR LESSONS ON BUILDING WEALTH

## Negative Beliefs about Wealth Attract Poverty

*The second key to* a life of triumph is building wealth.

Many people throughout the world face difficulties creating wealth. I have found that many people who are religiously inclined go through life believing in guilt-based perceptions about wealth. Whether they come from a Buddhist or a Christian background, many people believe that being wealthy will bar them from entering heaven in the afterlife. And because of how wealth and prosperity work, thinking of wealth as evil or unclean ends up attracting poverty instead of prosperity.

This perception of wealth also gives rise to another obstacle. When people fail to create wealth for themselves, they may feel jealous and critical of people who are wealthy and successful, and these feelings produce negative mental energy that creates a hell-like world within the mind.

This mental discord is the inevitable product of the self-chosen belief to oppose wealth. Some people prefer to remain detached from large amounts of money and other forms of abundance, but their hearts remain pure and unbounded by worldly desires. A life like this can be virtuous. But this can't be said of people who say that the wealthy are evil and deserve to suffer in hell. This kind of mindset produces a thick smog within the mind, creating a hellish space in one's inner world. This may seem odd at first, but it is really how our minds work. We stumble into a pitfall when the restrictions we set on our own lives lead us to judge and criticize others.

Another common pitfall that religious souls experience is an aversion to the opposite sex. Some people believe that getting married will lead them to hell in their afterlife. And perhaps some people *want* to believe this to be true. But in any case, the problems with wealth and the opposite sex are common stumbling blocks for religious souls.

## Wealth Can Be Used to Bring Happiness to Others

We can overcome a mindset that opposes wealth by understanding the vital purpose that it serves in this world. Wealth comes in many forms, such as money and assets, but why does it exist?

Wealth's purpose is to represent heaven's abundance in this world. Heaven is a world not of poverty, but of abundance of many splendid things. In addition, heaven is also governed by a spiritual law that grants the wishes of the pure of heart, allowing many inhabitants to live prosperously.

Since heaven's abundance cannot be expressed in this world, I believe that wealth is serving the role of representing it. Money isn't the only way that heaven's abundance is expressed in this world, but it is one of the ways.

From this perspective, we can see that many problems with wealth arise not from the nature of wealth itself, but from the motives, intentions, and objectives of the people who use it. The problem lies within our minds.

For example, money can be used for beneficial purposes. With money, a company can build an event hall to provide themselves with a venue for seminars, lectures, and conferences. And when these spaces are not being used, they can be lent out to other businesses and organizations that also need a venue for conferences.

Wealth can be used to benefit society in this way. The event hall helps other businesses and organizations by fulfilling a need, and the activities held there create joy and happiness for many of the people who attend them. In this way, wealth is an essential means for producing happiness in this world.

It is regrettable that wealth is a stumbling block for so

many people. If we want to make this world a better place to live, the virtuous and pure of heart need to be able to build wealth in virtuous ways and guide others to use their wealth virtuously and with good intentions. These things will make the world a better place for everyone.

I believe that wealth is a vital means of bringing happiness to a great number of people and that we should use it to construct an ideal world on Earth.

## Honest Poverty Is Toxic if It Gives Rise to Judgment and Envy

If you look within and discover that some part of you opposes wealth in your life or in the lives of others in a toxic way, you must fight and conquer that mindset. The problem with an aversion to wealth arises when it makes us feel righteous about trying to change other people's beliefs about wealth. There is nothing wrong with honest poverty, and if this is the way of life we want to follow, we have the right to choose it. But when we do, we need to be mindful not to allow it to give rise to envy or a judgmental attitude toward others.

If our decision to live in honest poverty allows us to remain detached from excessive material desire and maintain the purity of our hearts, then our state of impoverishment is producing goodness and virtue. In contrast, if our appreciation for honest poverty foments feelings of jealousy and resentment of others' wealth, then our state of impoverishment has clouded our hearts, and is, therefore, morally toxic.

There are many different values, beliefs, and ways of life in this world that don't deserve our criticism or judgment. Just as we have the right to choose lives of honest poverty, other people have the right to choose lives of prosperity. We have the right and the freedom to make our choices, but we don't have the right to expect others to make the same ones, nor do they deserve our jealousy or envy just because they choose differently.

Some wealthy people use their huge fortunes to create their own suffering. But wealth can also bring about a peace of mind that being impoverished or in debt cannot. Having enough financial freedom to liberate our lives from money-related distress is a good thing that allows us to live comfortably and free from the temptation of jealousy.

If our love of poverty is making us feel miserable and envious and is restricting our creativity and freedom, then it's best to make an effort to overcome this mindset and break free from it. I recommend that we make this a clear goal to achieve and set the further goal of making an effort to build wealth.

# The Three Basic Principles for Building Wealth

## THE FIRST PRINCIPLE
*Practicing Mindful Economy Is the First Step to Wealth*

There are three basic principles of building wealth. The first, tried and true principle is practicing economy in your spending. Practicing thrift and cutting out wasteful spending is the starting point of saving money. If we constantly overspend our wealth on lavish purchases, we'll eventually exhaust the valuable wealth we worked hard to build.

Failing at this first principle is the reason that many businesses and enterprises see "the third generation go back to the mill." The third generation of owners, which is more accustomed to a luxurious lifestyle than the first and second generations, often don't remember the hard work that it took their predecessors to build their businesses and succeed. They've lost the predecessors' work ethic and knowledge of how to spend wealth wisely, and as a result, they tend to use up their wealth wastefully on unnecessary expenditures, often bringing the enterprise to eventual ruin. This pitfall afflicts both large organizations and private lives.

Practicing economy is not the same as being miserly, however. Being miserly unfortunately does nothing to attract wealth. So the key to this principle is to treat your good fortune and wealth with a respectful attitude and not use your money wastefully.

## THE SECOND PRINCIPLE
*Wealth Gathers to Those Who Have a Purpose For It*

The second principle of building wealth is that wealth comes to those who know how to put it to good use. Wealth doesn't grow in places that don't have a purpose, such as the middle of a barren field.

For example, countless people put their wealth into banks. People entrust their money to banking institutions because they know how to use the wealth they are charged with: they lend it to businesses and other enterprises that have a purpose for it.

The same principle applies at the individual level. Let's imagine that your dream is to become a homeowner and you want to build a new home for you and your family. Because you have this clear goal in mind, you will work very hard to increase your income. Increasing your income will also be an essential goal if you have a large family with a lot of children and you want to send each of them to college. In both these examples, wealth is drawn to people who have a clear purpose.

An important step in creating wealth, then, is to have a clearly defined purpose for your wealth. Envision how you want to use your wealth and how much you will need to make that vision a reality. Without a clear use for your wealth, you may only be able to gather a very nominal amount.

There is an abundance of wealth all around the world, and it is looking for people who can make use of it. It is constantly gathering around those who demonstrate that they have the ability and knowledge to use it. In many ways, wealth is the blood that runs through our veins, working to carry oxygen and nutrients to the parts of our body that need nourishment.

Put another way, there are people around the world who have a lot of wealth but know that they aren't capable of putting it to good use and want to find someone with good ideas that they can fund. This is why people with good ideas receive a lot of capital flow from multiple contributors.

Setting up a new business is a common example of this. When we come up with a prosperous business idea, it moves the hearts of many people who want to support its actualization, and the more attention and energy it draws, the more wealth is attracted to it through means such as bank loans, joint ownership investments, or contributions of property.

In this way, wealth gathers around people who have the passion to realize a good idea—people who know how to put it to good use. And to recognize a good purpose, you need a philosophy that promotes wealth and prosperity.

# THE THIRD PRINCIPLE
*Those Who Give Shall Receive*

This leads us to the third principle of building wealth, which is the spiritual principle that those who give shall also receive. You should use the wealth you gather to achieve aims that benefit people's lives and bring them happiness, not to serve your own interests. By doing this, the wealth you give to others ultimately circulates back to you. Put more simply, the nature of wealth is that when you use it for your own sake, it tends to diminish, but when you use it for others' sake, it spreads and multiplies.

The famous American industrialist Henry Ford was an automobile magnate who succeeded in amassing a huge fortune in his lifetime. The driving force that led him to this achievement was his passionate desire to open the world to a new age in which the average businessman and factory worker could own his or her own car, and so could every other worker in the country. He dreamed of building an automobile that would be affordable to the average American worker, and he was able to make this dream a reality.

Konosuke Matsushita, the Japanese electronics tycoon and founder of Panasonic, is another shining example of a modern industrialist who achieved great wealth through an altruistic dream. He is famous for applying what he called the tap water philosophy to produce useful electrical appliances for the home at reasonable prices. His philosophy was based on the economics of how we perceive tap water. Tap water is not free, but there is such an inexhaustible supply that it is provided at a low cost—so low that if someone stopped by and washed their hands from your garden hose, you wouldn't consider them a thief. Since water is not completely without cost, this may be considered an act of theft in the strictest sense of the law. But because the tap water is supplied at minimal expense, no one would consider this a crime.

In the same way, Konosuke Matsushita dreamed of supplying Japan with low-cost electrical appliances so that households throughout the country would be able to buy them as easily as they would turn on their tap water. This philosophy was a philosophy of love that grew from his wish to supply his country with products that were useful for their lives. His philosophy led his company to huge success, eventually resulting in billions of dollars of profit and growth into a major international corporation.

The nature of how love and wealth work is that by giving them, you are also receiving them through a constant cycle of goodness. This cycle eventually generates tremendous reservoirs of wealth. Continuing to contribute to this cycle of love and wealth is what allows us to achieve infinite progress. This isn't the same as being charitable toward the unfortunate and needy; it is a different form of love that makes us want to find many ways to be of service to many kinds of people.

There are numerous other ways of building wealth, but the three principles I have described are the most basic and essential. First, we must use our wealth mindfully and practice economy. Second, we need to set a clear purpose for our wealth. And third, we should use our wealth with love and a desire to serve others. By following these three principles, you will amass a great fortune and a virtuous influence that will carry you through the gates of heaven in the afterlife.

# THREE LESSONS FOR A HAPPY MARRIAGE

## Cultivating Yourself Attracts Your Ideal Partner

*Choosing the ideal partner* to marry is a major life decision that many of us hope to make, but we could already be taking five, ten, or even twenty years to make this decision. There is a simple solution, but it may sound contrary to what you expect to hear and to your current ideas about finding an ideal match.

The truth about seeking your ideal partner is that chasing it zealously or searching for it eagerly doesn't lead you closer to it but leads you further away. This may sound perplexing, because we're often told that effort is always rewarded and that by asking we shall receive. So if you've been applying this perspective to the search for your ideal partner, you might think that I'm encouraging a wrong and pessimistic outlook.

I believe that both of these are Truths: if you ask, so shall you receive, and if you persevere, so shall your hard work be rewarded. Except it works slightly differently when the object of your desire is an ideal partner. In this particular situation, your wish to get married will most likely come true as long as you truly desire that to happen. But your wish to marry the person of your dreams is a desire that may not be granted.

This situation is a lot like puppies and kittens chasing after their own tails. A puppy can run and spin after its alluring tail as hard as it can without ever being rewarded for its effort. But as soon as it stops and starts to walk forward, the tail follows from behind with no effort. Finding your ideal spouse is strikingly similar.

Your spouse, as they say, is your "better half." Your spouse is an intrinsic part of your being, so the harder you pursue your ideal relationship, the more it will escape you. But, remarkably, when you stop and move forward with your life, the right partner will find you.

To find your ideal partner, I recommend two things as your starting point. My first piece of advice is to cultivate yourself so that you become someone that your ideal spouse would want to marry. If your ideal partner turned up in front of you right now, you would want him to feel that he's found his perfect match in you. This is why cultivating yourself should be your first priority. You might feel tempted to have a list of qualities you want the person of your dreams to have. But doing this won't help you find someone with all those qualities, because that person may not exist. However, you will increase your chances of success if you cultivate the qualities that your ideal partner would want in the person he or she hopes to marry.

The reason I recommend self-cultivation is that the most important condition you want to fulfill when you first get married is that you and your partner are a perfect match. A perfect fit is difficult to achieve when you're looking for someone to fit your image of a dream man or dream woman. And if you're not making the effort to cultivate yourself so that you'll be a good match for your ideal partner, chances are that he or she will pass you by like an express train.

Having a clear image in mind of your ideal partner and wishing to marry this kind of person is a good thing, but at the same time, you also need to examine how you'll be perceived from your partner's perspective. If your dream were to marry a very attractive movie star, and by chance, he came up to talk to you or put his arm around you, how would you react? You might feel extremely shy and embarrassed and try to flee the scene. If you were to react like this, it would be a clear sign to him that you aren't his match. To get your ideal partner to feel a connection with you, he or she also needs to feel that you are his or her perfect match.

You may be facing problems with indecision; perhaps you have been in a lot of relationships or have been introduced to a lot of people but are still unable to choose a partner. This, too, is about an inability to assess yourself objectively. Without a clear idea of who you are, it's difficult to think objectively about who will be a good match for you. You keep raising your sights and lowering them again in search of a partner, because everyone you meet seems to be a bad fit. If you develop a clear self-image and a good sense of where you want to go in your life, you'll be able to see potential partners objectively and recognize your ideal partner when he or she comes along.

For example, I recommend that you consider your career path when you're looking for a partner. If you have a job or career that you would like to continue pursuing, focus first on establishing yourself in your job or career, getting a clear sense of your prospects for financial success, and planning out how you would like to live in the future. This will help you see yourself objectively. When you know clearly what kind of company, industry, or career path you want to pursue, where you want to be in the future, what your current income is, and what you will earn in the future, and you are also passionate about this vision, you can be certain that your ideal partner will appear. And once you have a clear, objective vision of what your own future holds, you'll be able to be decisive in your choice of a partner.

On the other hand, if you see marriage as no more than a fallback so you can quit your job without risking financial insecurity or see your job only as a way to attract prospective partners, this won't help you find your ideal partner. This is the way our lives work.

## A Deep, Empathic Connection
## Is the Key to a Lasting Marriage

The second key to finding your ideal partner is to look for someone with whom you feel an empathic connection. Among all the conditions you should fulfill when choosing someone to marry, this is the most essential.

There are so many conditions we want to consider in choosing our marriage partners that we can easily get confused. Should we look for partners who are beautiful or average-looking? Tall or short? Thick-boned or skinny? Financially well-off and academically intelligent, or neither?

We can look for any number of desirable qualities, but it's rare to find someone who has all of them. So we each have to be prepared to choose someone who doesn't meet every one of our conditions—but then we face the challenge of figuring out which qualities are most important. For example, perhaps we're choosing between the person who has an impeccable academic background but is not yet financially stable, the person with a pretty face who's the wrong height, and the guy or girl who has the best looks but doesn't have the smarts you're looking for.

It's a tough decision to make, so we go to our friends and family to ask for their input—but that ends up making things even more complicated. One friend may tell you that marriage lasts longer with a partner that's beautiful, while another may tell you that it's a risk to choose someone who's too physically attractive and it's much more important to choose based on personality. Still others may say that intelligence is most essential or that financial background makes the biggest difference in a marriage.

So what is the most important thing we should look for in our ideal spouse? As a general rule, I recommend that you choose someone with whom you feel a deep empathic connection. Being financially established now doesn't guarantee a well-off future, someone with a good-natured personality might have a difficult side that you haven't noticed yet, and you might get used to attractive looks. What remains in an ideal relationship after all the fleeting components are stripped away is a deep connection of mutual understanding.

At the beginning, a marriage based on just the external, superficial conditions you were looking for might appear to work. But in a marriage like that, the connection between you and your partner is likely to weaken over time. When these external aspects change, the two of you will grow apart. But a marriage based on deep mutual empathy between two people is bound to last for decades.

For example, there are probably many people who decided to marry their spouses because of their accomplished academic backgrounds, but sometimes people who studied hard in school end up changing once they begin working in the real world. Instead of continuing to learn, they begin drinking themselves into a stupor whenever they're at home. Their spouses expected a very different lifestyle and are probably shocked and disappointed. It's a fact that many people change over time, and the person you choose may not turn out to be the person they seemed to be at the beginning of a marriage.

If you are thinking about basing your decision of who to marry on academic status, keep in mind that a strong record of achievement at school doesn't necessarily equal true or lasting intelligence. The correlation is probably about 60 to 70 percent but definitely doesn't reach 100 percent. In fact, many people who are truly intelligent don't necessarily do well in school. A person's intelligence is determined more by inner aptitude, so some intelligent people may not do well in school but grow into genuine intellectuals as they mature into their thirties, forties, fifties, and so on. On the other hand, if a person was forced to do well in school but didn't have genuine interest in cultivating their intelligence, they'll find it hard to continue to learn as they grow older. These are sometimes the people who end up drowning themselves in alcohol and bringing their lives to ruin.

Many factors seem important when choosing a spouse, but if you were to make a decision based on the one most important condition, you would choose someone you feel a deep empathic connection with, someone whose outlook on life resonates with yours and who you can see yourself walking alongside on the same journey of life.

And if you want to continue to build your career throughout your marriage, you should also gauge how much your partner understands the value you place on your work life. If, in your heart, you feel very confident that he or she supports and appreciates your career life, this is a strong sign that your marriage will most likely be filled with happiness.

## A Perfect Union Is Built Together Over Time

Finally, I would like to touch on how to build a lasting, successful marriage. The beginning of a marriage is a period of happiness, but many marriages these days break down later on and end in separations. Many people think that marriage partners are supposed to fit each other like a lock and key, so that by marrying the perfect fit they're guaranteed a successful, happy marriage, and if something goes wrong, it must mean they chose the wrong person. In some ways, adopting this perspective means seeing a human being as an object—your spouse becomes something that will either succeed or fail at making you happy. People with this perspective blame their marriage problems on having chosen the wrong partner. Adopting this perspective makes it more likely that a marriage will end in failure; certainly, going into a marriage with this mindset inevitably leads to problems down the road.

Every marriage is a work in progress as each strives to become the other's ideal match. We're all human, and no two people start out as such a perfect union that they never need to change or work on anything. Marriage is a coming together of two people who feel they have a good chance at happiness together and vow to build a strong union on their new journey together.

When we face tough times with each other, we can think of what we can do to strengthen our bond. We can search for ideas and ways to fill in the gaps between us. If we muster the will and effort to understand each other deeply, we may find our perseverance helps us build a better union, and rise up stronger from the hardest crises that are a part of the journey of marriage.

# 5

# THREE LESSONS FOR FINDING PEOPLE WHO CAN CHANGE YOUR DESTINY

## Your Strong Desire Will Lead You to the Person Who Holds the Key to Your Future

*Some people touch our* lives only briefly but in that time are able to point us to our path of happiness. These are the special people who open our lives to a brighter destiny, and every moment we have with them should be cherished.

If you are around the age of twenty, you may or may not have met one or two people who played a defining role in the direction your life has taken so far. But if you're thirty or older, you might look back at the turning points in your life and remember that they often involved people who changed your destiny. When we look back, it seems that each time we needed to decide which path to take—the one on the left, the one on the right, or the one straight ahead—we had someone to help us. And our acceptance of their influence became the deciding factor in the course of our future.

When we're faced with moments as critical as turning points, our hope is that we'll meet people who can point us in a positive direction. But, of course, there are times when the opposite happens and, to our dismay, we are led into a downward spiral of failure. Some people have had the unfortunate experience of being tricked into a bad business investment or of being betrayed. Some students have suffered from taking the bad advice of their guidance counselors during their college admissions.

In this section, however, I would like to talk about the people who influence us to choose brighter destinies. In China, there is a concept of a "noble person"; traditionally, the noble person represents someone from an aristocratic background or someone who has a high social status, but the term is used broadly to refer to anyone who has a stronger education, greater virtue, or more wealth than you do. This concept is sometimes used in common greetings in China: instead of saying, "How are you doing?" or "How have you been?" they actually say, "Have you met a noble person recently?"

I believe that meeting people of greater wisdom or influence can bring great changes to our lives. The principal teachings in my philosophy are based on the spirit of self-reliance, and practicing this spirit is the key to making our way up the staircase of life, one step at a time. In comparison, meeting a special person can resemble using an elevator along the way. It can lift you many stories higher in a matter of seconds, and when you're there, you are suddenly introduced to a completely new world. Moments like these are scattered throughout everyone's lives.

Put another way, there are people in our lives who open our destiny and whose words have the power to guide us through major turning points. What they say to us might not come out of any deep thought or serious consideration, and later on they might not even remember what they said to us—but somehow their words held the key to a brighter destiny. When we decide to listen to the advice and opinions of these people, it can illuminate our lives and change our lives forever.

Each and every person will go through this experience. Just when these people will come into our lives differs from person to person. But they will come to you if you continue to wish it to happen and hold an earnest intention of cherishing each encounter with them.

If you look back at your life and can't remember having had these moments, it's most likely because you've forgotten about them, have not been appreciative of them, or have been oblivious to the fact that they led you to make great leaps. If you think hard enough in search of them you are certain to discover that you, too, have had these experiences.

The more prepared you are to have this kind of encounter, the greater the likelihood is that it will happen. So, at the beginning of each new year or each new month, prepare your mind with a strong anticipation that someone will offer you advice that will lead you in a positive direction. Whether this wish comes true or not depends on the strength of your own anticipation.

A strong desire encourages your guardian and guiding angels to try to make it come true. When they feel your strong determination to reach such a commendable objective, they are inspired to find that special person for you. Thus, sometimes you meet the special person directly, and other times invisible beings are actively aiding the actualization of your wishes.

Wherever they are, there are people who are watching over you with supportive eyes, wishing to lend you their aid. Your earnest desire is the most essential factor in bringing these people's support to you.

## Humbleness Opens Your Mind to Other People's Advice

In addition to having a strong wish for special people to come into our lives, we also need to keep our hearts humbly opened to the words of those who are wiser than us. It's important that we acknowledge in our hearts that many people have the wisdom of a higher perspective than ours and to mindfully keep our ears open to other people's words so as not to let any precious advice slip past us. We need to be always on the lookout for people and advice that hold the keys to changing our lives.

We should also do the best we can not to miss their precious advice. We don't want to waste our valuable moments with them by letting them slip by. So if a voice within you says that the person in front of you is your goddess of happiness or the goddess of good fortune, don't let this moment pass you by. You need to make the most of this chance that's being offered to you.

Meetings with the special people who change our destiny are the most important events in our lives. They are our precious, most shining moments. These are the moments when we find ourselves standing at the crossroads of destiny with all kinds of people preparing to lend us their hands to help us open the path to a bright future.

Believing that you can bring such a change to your life on your own is a big mistake. Such a change always requires the help and support of others. This is the reason we need to remain humble and open-minded. You may have expected me to talk more about self-reliance as the key to achieving continuous victory through life's challenges, but gaining the help of others is actually one of the true paths to success in life.

In these moments, many people offer us opportunities. When many people want to help you further your goals and bring you success, it's difficult not to succeed. It's as if you're riding a wave of success. By contrast, when a lot of people are trying to hinder you from succeeding, it's far more difficult to do and requires much more effort.

To sum up, we do not achieve success by our own efforts alone. It is important to always remember that it is through the help of others that we are able to achieve our goals.

## Gratitude Is the Key to Our Success in Life

I would be lying if I were to say that I didn't work hard to get to where I am today, but the reason I was able to walk the path I did is because I received the support of a large number of people, and even more from divine providence.

In the usual terms, I suppose some may describe this as my "luck," but for someone like me who knows firsthand about divine power, it is impossible to use the word "luck." I know that my success is the result of the cooperation of divine spirits in heaven, and it is because of their very real work that I have been blessed with such good fortune.

For this reason, I believe that gratitude is very important

to our success in life. When our fortunes take a turn for the better, it's important that we not forget to express our gratitude to all those who supported us.

# 6

# TWO LESSONS FOR CREATING A SPIRITUAL LEGACY

## Virtue Is the Spiritual Legacy of True Success

*The fifth and final* piece of advice I would like to share is to create a spiritual legacy. In the previous sections, I discussed the first four keys to living a life of success: maintaining your body's balance and vitality, building wealth, finding an ideal partner, and meeting people who can change your life.

Depending on how you understand these four keys, you might see them as primarily about material success. But to be truly successful, we need more than worldly achievements—our success needs to transcend the material gains that we reap here on Earth.

What helps us attain true victory in this world? It is the happiness that our success brings us—the sort of happiness we can take with us to the other world. What sort of happiness is that? It is the spiritual happiness that elevates our success to a level that transcends this world. Put another way, it is the eternal treasures we cultivate from our heart.

If you have been introduced to my teachings of the Truths before, you probably already know that creating a spiritual legacy—an accomplishment far greater than worldly success alone—is an indispensable element in attaining true success in life.

Calling it a spiritual legacy may sound abstract, so if I were to give it another name, I would call it virtue. An innate talent is an ability we are born with, so it is something we have possessed since birth. Whether or not our talents are given a chance to grow and blossom, the seeds are there from the day we arrive into this world, and it is up to us to develop this potential. Virtue, on the other hand, is an aspect of our character that we all need to acquire through effort throughout our lives in this world. Even the souls of angels and other sacred divinities who become incarnated on Earth do not begin their lives already virtuous. They have the innate gifts that their souls carry with them, but to cultivate virtue, even they need to persevere.

# Virtue Is Cultivated through
# Both Adversity and Success

We develop our virtuous character over many decades. How do we do this?

Two kinds of circumstances foster virtue. One is when we are in the midst of setbacks, failure, and adversity; the other is when we are in the midst of success. These are the times when we can most easily develop virtue. Of course, we can become virtuous at other times in our lives, but the great virtue that stands as a monument to our life's achievements arises from these two experiences.

Let's explore why our virtue grows through times of adversity, failure, and setback. It is common for people to complain when they're suffering through adversity, because they are unable to endure its pressures. When they make a mistake, they're apt to lay the blame on someone else, the environment, or their own bad luck. We can say that this is a reaction we find in the average person.

Others who have achieved a slightly higher state of consciousness do not allow themselves to be crushed under adversity but instead try to accept it for what it is and endure it. People who try to bear their misfortune in this way have developed a stronger state of mind than the average. Beyond that are people who strive to always be optimistic and happy, despite the adversity they face. These people can be said to stand on the bottom rungs of a higher level of consciousness.

However, the people who are truly to be admired are those who use invincible thinking to counteract all adversity. When faced with misfortune, they are able to detect the divine intention within it and ask themselves what this affliction is supposed to teach them. They don't let the precious chance to learn a lesson escape them. They read the divine intention in their predicament and ask themselves what it is that they need to develop, what this adversity is trying to teach them, and use their answers as bases for building their characters or as principles underpinning their actions. People who go through such experience develop an extraordinarily strong degree of virtue that radiates light.

Enduring hardship and despair is in itself remarkable, but truly extraordinary people read the divine will behind their experience, search within it for some seed that will lead them to success, and nurture this seed. The inner strength needed to do this makes a person truly extraordinary, and this is how virtue is really born.

The second kind of circumstance that gives rise to virtue involves success. People whose names go down in history have achieved great things in their lives. No matter how many times they may have failed, they ultimately achieved success. Take

Abraham Lincoln, for example. He suffered defeat in many elections, failed in personal relationships, and lost his fiancée to death, but he still went on to become the president of the United States and left a great legacy for his nation. Had he not become president, he would not have been remembered as one of the giants of American history. The virtuous go through successions of setbacks, but eventually they have a chance to bloom.

When success finally comes, the mindset with which we handle our accomplishment is very important for fostering the growth of our virtue. We must not try to claim the fruits of success for ourselves. Rather, it's important that we remember that we succeeded not by our own efforts alone, but through the will of heaven. Although we were the ones who give the seed water and fertilizer, the seed's full potential was present when it was offered to us. We only helped it blossom of its own accord. This is how we should regard our successes. An attitude of not turning our successes into personal achievements is what gives rise to great personal virtue.

But if, instead, we consider our achievements to be all ours and believe that they came about solely as a result of our own efforts and skills, this mindset will hinder our virtue from developing; in this case, we will only be able to succeed by using our talents or inborn abilities.

In contrast, what will happen if we give the credit to the efforts and support of other people? What will be the result, if we believe that our success comes from the will of our guardian and guiding angels and the sacred divinities of heaven? When we perceive our successes in this way, it inspires us to use them for the benefit of as many people as possible. This is how we develop a virtuous mind.

No matter how unique our lives are, we can always cultivate our virtue in times of adversity and times of success, and this virtue becomes our spiritual legacy. We cultivate this spiritual treasure within our heart, and it will remain with us when we return to the other world. This is how we all can live a life of true victory.

Chapter Four

# THE POWER OF
# Invincible
# Thinking

# LINKING SELF-REFLECTION AND PROGRESS

*Conventional positive thinking* focuses on the bright side of things and takes a constructive view on everything, disregarding any negative aspects or the dark side of things. It teaches that even if we make a mistake or fail, the best thing to do is not let it bother us and keep moving forward positively and constructively. While this is a very powerful philosophy, one downside may be that it does not leave room for self-reflection, which is about reviewing and correcting your thoughts, words, and actions.

Positive thinking seems to contradict the principle of self-reflection because these two ideas seem to point in opposite directions, leaving us baffled about which path to take. I used to think it was best to leave it up to the individual to decide which method was right for them. But on seeing the confusion this caused for some people, I decided to introduce invincible thinking, which is the idea that connects these two seemingly opposing ideas.

Invincible thinking links the principles of self-reflection and progress, both of which are part of my four Principles of Happiness—love, wisdom, self-reflection, and progress. Invincible thinking is an all-around mindset that gives you the power to solve any problem that you otherwise wouldn't know what to do about.

No matter how positive and constructive our attitude may be, there are times when we face failures and setbacks. But ignoring these problems or telling ourselves that everything will be all right because we are essentially children of light won't necessarily solve them, because our minds are not that simple.

When we look within and explore our mind, we come to see that the human mind is not made to follow a single pattern of thinking. Each one of us has a depth in our heart and mind that gives rise to unique feelings and ideas, and invincible thinking serves the variety of profound thoughts that we each have as unique individuals.

Each of us can use invincible thinking in the way that best suits our needs, but I strongly feel that I should offer some guidance on the approach and the methods we should use. It is in this light that I would like to talk about the power of invincible thinking.

# SOLVING PROBLEMS IN THE PHYSICAL WORLD

*Invincible thinking is based* on the idea that we are all bound to fail at some point in life. No one can sail through life without any problems or setbacks. We fall to one side, then to the other, go up and down, tumble over, and stand up again numerous times in life. By going through a variety of good and bad experiences, we are searching for ways to improve our life and walk the path to happiness. So how can we, as the ones facing this reality, live through our time in this world? Invincible thinking offers an answer to this question.

Invincible thinking is probably the most powerful attitude in this three-dimensional physical world, the environment in which we live and work now. In the other world, which consists of the fourth dimension and beyond, different principles are at work. For instance, we can manifest almost 100 percent of our latent power to become what we want to become based on the spiritual laws of the will. But it doesn't necessarily work the same way in the material world, because each one of us is at a different stage of the journey of manifesting our potential. Similarly, the idea that only light is true existence holds true in the higher dimensions of the spirit world, but evil does exist in the three-dimensional world. Invincible thinking is a principle that bridges this world and the other and offers a clear guideline for solving any outstanding issues from the perspective of this physical world.

# 3

# TRANSFORMING DIFFICULTIES INTO NOURISHMENT FOR THE SOUL

*Invincible thinking is based* on the idea that all difficulties in life can be turned into nourishment for the soul. We all face setbacks, failures, and difficulties over the course of our lives, but simply ignoring or avoiding them won't truly serve us. If you ponder deeply why you were born into this world in the first place, you'll realize that it certainly wasn't to avoid hardships and adversities.

We human beings are given the chance to be born into this world once every few hundred or few thousand years to gain experiences in different environments and to meet new people. The experiences that we go through are not necessarily all pleasant, but we were all well aware of this before we were born here. We knew that our life wouldn't always be smooth sailing, because the purpose of being born into this world is to improve our character and strengthen our inner light by accumulating various experiences and learning through trial and error.

This spiritual perspective—that human beings have eternal life and are repeatedly born into this world in a cycle of reincarnation—will allow us to recognize all the events and experiences that we encounter in this world as invaluable treasures for our souls. When we look at our lives from this grand perspective, we begin to see difficulties and hardships in a new light. This perspective is the basis of invincible thinking.

What will ultimately determine whether you have triumphed in life is how you have coped with and striven to overcome your difficulties and challenges, using all your knowledge, skills, and ideas, and how much you were able to transform these hardships into the strength of your soul. We should never be complacent with a life without any hardships or difficulties. As I often say, life is like a workbook of problems to solve, and each one of us has to find the answers for the problems in our own workbook.

So to practice invincible thinking, we need to first acknowledge that we ourselves have to solve the problems in own workbook of life; no one else can do this for us. As we find solutions to each of the problems we face, we can begin to help and guide others as they work to solve the problems in their workbook. At the same time, our efforts will give us greater understanding that we can use to produce positive and constructive outcomes for our society and the larger world. This is the basic framework of invincible thinking.

# 4

# MASTERING
# OUR TIME IN LIFE

*Since founding Happy Science*, I have met and talked to a large number of people who have had many different views. Taking part in this new movement had changed the lives of many of them in some way or another. Some had come under a spotlight, while others had faded away while going though ups and downs. Each person had their own story to tell, however small it seemed to them.

In the course of a lifetime, we go through various experiences, some good and others bad. Some bring us happiness and others unhappiness, and things don't always go the way we want them to. If we look at how people deal with various situations, we can categorize them into the following two groups.

People in the first group make smooth progress when things are going their way, like a yacht sailing in a tailwind, but as soon as they find themselves facing a headwind, they can no longer move forward, and they go under like a capsized or sunken ship.

Many people fall into this category.

The other group of people stands at the opposite end of the first group. With indomitable spirits, they show us how strong, pure, and persistent their initial desires were as they face both favorable and adverse situations. In fact, an indomitable spirit is an essential attitude we need to cultivate to be truly empowered by invincible thinking. We all get excited about new ideas, but the authenticity of our wishes can be proven in the passage of time.

Invincible thinking allows us to be the master of our own time; it lets us triumph over time and have it in our power. To see whether you are using the power of invincible thinking, reflect back on yourself six months ago, a year ago, two years ago, and three years ago. Compared to your present self, can you track the progress you have made, or do you see yourself regressing? We need to constantly check whether we are staying on or straying from the right path. When you look back over the path you have taken, if you see a single track of steady progress, then you have been winning the bigger battle of life, even if you have suffered numerous losses in everyday matters.

A person with invincible thinking is like a tree that keeps growing even amid numerous difficulties and hardships. Sometime, a strong wind may blow and strip the branches of the leaves. The tree may come close to dying from a lack of sufficient nourishment, or a wild animal may come dig in the ground, ruining its roots. But no matter what happens, the tree strives to keep growing steadily toward the sky. Invincible thinking is the power that helps us make this kind of persistent and continuous effort.

# 5

# GROWING STRONG
# LIKE BAMBOO

*Invincible thinking allows us* to grow in both the good times and bad times of life, in something of the same way that bamboo grows. Bamboo grows very tall and straight. It's tough enough to withstand harsh environments and flexible enough to bend in every direction.

If you look closely, you'll notice that a bamboo's trunk is divided into many joints, or nodes; each joint marks the end of a cell; and each cell is typically eight to twelve inches long. The trunk is thick on the bottom, and as it grows, it gradually becomes thinner and softer, as we can see from the way it bends in the wind. Over time, however, the thin, weak parts grow stronger, which helps the bamboo grow taller.

I am impressed by the steady way that bamboo grows, and it makes me think of the effort that bamboo plants put into creating joints. The joints are what make bamboo unique: they allow bamboo to grow very tall, typically reaching more than a hundred feet, while remaining resistant to stiff winds. No matter how strong the wind, bamboo will not break easily. Although bamboo is not a massive tree, it will not break or snap easily, and this shows how resilient it is.

The wind may blow, and the rain may fall, but bamboo just keeps on growing regardless—and the number of joints is the proof of its growth. I sometimes wonder how the bamboo might feel as it creates each of its joints. I am sure it feels a sense of fulfillment from knowing how much it has grown.

Unlike bamboos, persimmons look sturdy and do not sway or bend, but they can actually be quite weak and snap easily. Willow is another tree that looks weedy but is flexible and truly strong. Bamboo looks fragile—its diameter is typically only eight to ten inches. But a bamboo shoot comes out of the ground and grows steadily to become a tall, flexible, yet strong plant.

Like bamboo, each of us may appear fragile. But we can construct our lives to resemble how bamboos grow: with flexibility and strength in harmony. Both of these qualities are essential. We should be tough but not rigid so that we can cope with all kinds of situations. We should aim to live this way because this physical world that we live in now is no hothouse: rain falls and winds blow. Sometimes, we may be hit by snowstorms or stricken by drought.

Just as bamboos go through a cycle of creating joints and stalks, our lives seem to have cycles, and fortune's wheel turns around periodically. I cannot say how many years or months each cycle lasts, but one thing is certain: we experience both good times and bad times in turn.

At the turning points in our life, we always experience difficulty coping with our current circumstances or with the people around us, which causes us mental anguish. But this doesn't mean that our lives would be better without hardships and adversities, because these are the times when wonderful things start happening to us. We see that difficult experiences nourish our souls and teach us the most important lessons in life. With this perspective, we no longer have to fear failures and setbacks. Times of adversity mark the beginning of a truly exciting life.

Adversity is like the time when a bamboo plant makes a new joint. This must be a painful time for the bamboo; after growing smoothly and steadily for eight to twelve inches, it reaches the point where it needs to create a joint. The bamboo probably wishes it could just continue growing smoothly in the same way for thirty or even sixty feet, but it has to stop growing to create a new joint every eight to twelve inches. I am sure it suffers a feeling of resistance and stagnation when it can no longer grow as it pleases. It must feel as if it's being inhibited by an uncontrollable force.

The bamboo suffers pain and confusion, feeling as if it has reached a plateau, but soon the energy wells up inside to create a new joint. Once it forms a new node, the bamboo can grow smoothly again until it has to stop to make another one. This time of stagnation is probably painful for the bamboo, but it is necessary for it to keep growing continuously, as its joints become the basis for further growth.

Similarly, fortune's wheel turns around in cycles, bringing good times and bad, luck and misfortune to our lives. But going through this cycle is how we can build foundations for the future and grow from there, in the same way that the bamboo creates nodes to grow stalks. Times of adversity are the joints in our lives; they facilitate further growth and let us advance to the next stage.

Look back over your past, and ponder the time when you learned the deepest life lessons. It may have been when you were hurt by someone's words or when you failed in business, went bankrupt, or fell ill. Whatever the setbacks you've experienced, when you look back on them five or ten years later, you will find that they have become the most memorable moments of your life. So whenever you face difficulties, tell yourself that you are in the middle of creating a joint that will let you move forward to the next stage on the path of growth.

# 6

## ACHIEVING STEADY GROWTH IN A HARSH ENVIRONMENT

*When I was a child*, I built a homemade incinerator so I could burn rubbish in our backyard. I placed bricks and stones around the fire to keep it from spreading. A tree stood near the incinerator, and I thought the heat would kill it. But contrary to my expectation, the tree not only survived but also got tougher and tougher. It continued to grow, even when other trees died.

Life next to the incinerator must have been very harsh for that tree. Nevertheless, the tree kept growing, leaving its growth marks in its annual rings. It was full of life, and its trunk grew progressively thicker. Strangely enough, another tree, one that was growing in the most favorable environment, was easily knocked down by a strong wind in a typhoon. This fallen tree reminds me of someone who got on the fast track of life, someone who was born into a wealthy family and has lived his whole life in comfort, but as soon as an unfavorable wind blows, he falls down, unable to bear the situation.

On the other hand, someone who continues to grow and build strength despite a harsh environment does not give in easily. The ability to endure hardships enables us to get through any difficulty in life; it helps us grow like a tree with rings left by the seasons of its life, and it turns us into people of great stature.

The biographies of great historical figures often tell of the hardships they weathered. This is because enduring adverse circumstances over the course of our life in this world is essential to accumulating experiences for our soul. I myself have been through difficult times, but I was able to transform these experiences into the strength and wisdom that I now share with others to help them solve their problems.

We can develop resistance and immunity against adversities by exposing our bodies and souls to the buffeting winds of misfortune and the heat and snow of tribulation. This experience gives us knowledge and skills that we can use to overcome life's problems. Once we acquire our own know-how to cope with difficult situations, we can develop new perspectives by considering any new knowledge we gain, as well as the experiences of others, in light of our own experience. Every skill and piece of knowledge we gain eventually becomes our own life lesson and transforms into a powerful energy for the soul.

# 7

# THINKING LONG-TERM
# TO WIN IN THE END

*In addition to* an indomitable spirit, another essential habit to cultivate is seeing things from both short-term and long-term perspectives.

Taking a long-term perspective does not mean that we neglect what is happening in the present moment. Even if we've prepared ourselves for the winter by stocking up wood and coal, it doesn't mean we can do nothing and idle away our time until the winter comes. If it's summer now, there must be things we can and should do to live fully in this time of year.

But at times we feel that things could not possibly get worse and that there is no way we can endure any more hardship or misery. This is when we need to change our perspective completely; we should take a long-term perspective and remember that tough times only last for a short period of time. From a short-term perspective of one or two years, it may seem as if things didn't turn out the way we wanted them to. But a failure may simply mean that we did not succeed in the short term, and it does not necessarily mean we don't have the potential to succeed. So maybe we're not a sprinter, but maybe we're a good long-distance runner. Short-distance races are not the only competition; we can also compete in long-distance races. Similarly, we should measure our success not only in the short term, but also over the long term.

I've learned this from my own experience. When I was in high school, I ran a marathon and was able to finish the race as one of the top runners. I was never a fast runner, but I was able to pace myself successfully. At the beginning of the race, I joined a group of runners who had about the same level of running ability. As I ran with the group for a while, my body started warming up, which made me feel like I could run a little faster. So at about the halfway point, I began to pick up my pace and started running faster, feeling as if my legs had grown longer. From then on, I started running even faster, overtaking even someone who had beaten me in short-distance sprints.

Sprinters are usually muscular, and they often pace themselves wrong and get exhausted in the middle of long-distance races. They cannot keep up their pace for long and drop out halfway, panting and pausing for rest. This is why I was able to catch up to a sprinter in a long-distance race. He probably didn't expect it; he had a surprised look on his face as I approached him. He tried running faster to stay ahead of me, but he couldn't keep up and dropped behind. I could hardly believe what was happening, and this experience left a strong impression on me.

From this experience I learned the importance of pacing myself. And to do that, we need to assess our strength objectively and use that knowledge to achieve the best possible overall result. And pacing ourselves appropriately for our task is one area where we can always improve.

# 8

## ACCUMULATING EFFORT TO POWER OUR LIVES FORWARD

*Some people may be* struggling to enhance their learning ability. They may feel distressed because they don't have the time to read books or they have trouble memorizing things. In the short run, it is true that we have differences in ability. For instance, if several people are asked to master a new skill over the course of a year, some will master it sooner than others. But the purpose of our life is not to achieve a spiritual awakening in a year, nor to leave this world within one year. We are born here to nurture our souls and improve our characters as much as we can before we return to the other world.

When we become impatient and try to achieve something quickly, we often fail. But when we take a long-term perspective, we begin to see other options. We can't always assess someone's ability or measure their achievements within the limited time of one year or even three or four years. So why not make long-range life plans? By shifting our perspective this way, we can continue our endeavors even when others get tired and give up after a year or two.

When we think like long-distance runners, we will start seeing unexpected results. Strangely enough, we will find ourselves achieving our goals much faster, as if we were sprinters. The secret is the cumulative effect of all the efforts we have been making until now. You may not possess special skills or extraordinary ability. You may even feel frustrated with your inability, but if you persevere in your effort, you will start seeing a cumulative effect in your outcomes. After accumulating a certain amount of diligent effort, you will be able to achieve something much more quickly than you did before. This is a truly amazing experience.

Japanese sake is produced by letting a mixture of yeast and rice stand for a while to ferment. In the same way, the experiences and knowledge that we accumulate come to fruition after a period of time—usually when we least expect it. It seems that it takes a certain number of years for our efforts to bear fruit and power us forward.

We can see a similar process with other food and beverages; for example, wine increases in value when it's stored for years. Another example is dried bonito. We can certainly eat this fish fresh, but to make good dried bonito, it needs to be sun-dried and fermented. This aging process adds a nice taste to the fish. Things that are allowed to stand for a certain period of time can one day transform completely.

In terms of study habits, I believe there are roughly two types of people. The first type reads books from cover to cover, word by word, from the preface to the postscript. The other type focuses on and studies only certain parts of the book, picking out the sections they think are likely to be tested and skimming the rest. In the short term, people using the second approach can achieve their desired results quickly, and their technique seems effective. People who use the first approach, meticulously studying the textbook over and over again to deepen their understanding, may not see the results of their effort until much later. In the short term, they may even feel that they are not intelligent enough and fear that they lack the ability to achieve their goals. But in the end, the years of groundwork they've laid will bring about remarkable results and help them achieve self-realization, because they've put so much effort into developing an overall grasp of the material.

Even if we are not adroit at what we do, we should never give up. If we stop making an effort, that will be the end of it. But if we continue to strive, we will eventually break through the surface. What makes us keep going is willpower; we need to keep telling ourselves that we will not stay behind and that by the time we come out on top, we will have advanced significantly.

The same principle is at work in children's studies. The speed or rate of children's progress may vary, and their parents may look at their short-term academic records in primary or middle school and determine their children's potential prematurely. But there is one thing we should keep in mind: good grades in school do not guarantee success in life.

Children who get good grades often focus only on the main points of the lesson or study in advance for the next term. High achievers often know things they haven't been taught in class and can answer difficult questions, so they look smarter than the rest of the class. But their pattern of thinking is like the thinking of people who use credit cards to do all their shopping. They don't have any cash, so they charge everything and make payments later, when they get their paycheck. It's like they are living on debt.

Those who gain information ahead of time do well in the short term. In the same way, those who can make good, calculated guesses often score highly on exams. If they are blessed with a good partner or a favorable working environment, they may get ahead in life. But even if they experience temporary success, that doesn't indicate their real ability, because their success always depends on the type of people they work with or on the circumstances they work in. Getting the gist of things may seem like a smart thing to do in the short run, but it doesn't truly serve us in the long run.

Those who continue their efforts, no matter what kind of environment they are in and no matter who they work with, can achieve good results consistently. This is how the accumulation of hard work bears fruit.

Some of the knowledge we gain may not be absolutely necessary in life; this is what I refer to as an "unnecessary necessity." Not all information you learn in school gets tested in exams, but it is the students who study everything thoroughly who consistently achieve above a certain level no matter what their circumstance. These are the kinds of people who eventually achieve greatness.

# 9

# PREPARING FOR
# THE NEXT STEP

*It is quite possible* and relatively simple to make short-term profits in business. For instance, if you develop a unique product that no other business sells, offer free gifts, or introduce a new model, your product could become an instant hit. But it would most likely lose its popularity after a short time, resulting in a drop in sales. Lucrative businesses always attract competitors who imitate the original product or service. Even if the business thrives at the beginning, competition in the market may cause its decline.

Suppose you are in the hotel business and find a good site in the heart of the city where there are no other hotels nearby. You decide to build a hotel, and just as you expected, you make a handsome profit. However, you may soon find yourself in trouble if your competitors start building hotels in the same area.

In the hotel business, when the occupancy ratio exceeds 80 percent, rival companies come into the market. If you manage to fill more than 80 percent of your rooms, it means that there is a demand, so other hotel chains will open their own establishments nearby. As soon as a new hotel opens in the same area, your thriving business may see a sharp drop in sales. On the other hand, when the occupancy rate falls below 70 percent, your business goes below the break-even point and goes in the red. So your aim, in that case, would be to maintain an occupancy rate somewhere between 70 and 80 percent.

If we start a new business solely relying on the novelty of the product or service, our business is doomed to failure and decline. We should take on challenges that no one else has tried before, but when we achieve a certain level of success, we need to prepare for the next stage.

In the case of hotel management, generating repeat business is crucial to ensuring management stability. What makes your guests want to come back to your hotel again is high-quality service. If there are no other hotels in the area, you may be able to fill 80 to 90 percent of your rooms regardless of the quality of the service you offer. But if you don't improve your service, you will eventually lose your business when another hotel with better service is built nearby. Offering good-quality service that makes the guest want to return is vital for survival in the hotel business.

Sometimes we are blessed with fortunate circumstance or things work to our advantage, as if in answer to our prayers.

We may get lucky more often than we expect, but we should not depend on luck to bring success. We may as well enjoy any good fortune that comes our way, but we should at the same time start preparing for the next step.

Whether our circumstances are fortunate or unfortunate, whether the economy is good or bad, we need to continue offering a high-quality product or service so we can maintain a strong success rate. This is a simple but extremely important attitude that we should all try to develop.

# 10

## SOWING THE SEEDS OF LOVE IN FAVORABLE CIRCUMSTANCES

*I have talked about* the attitude we need to cultivate in the face of adversity. In times of adversity, we are given an opportunity to look deep within. We become introspective and have the luxury of examining our inner self. These are the times when we train and correct ourselves so we can improve. But it makes sense to adopt a different attitude when our circumstances change.

What, then, should we do when our circumstances are favorable? When everything goes exactly the way we hoped, we may feel that we don't need to practice invincible thinking and think that there's nothing more we need to do. But this is exactly when we are at risk of falling into a trap.

In times of prosperity, we should practice giving love. When luck is on our side, we should be doing something more than simply benefiting ourselves. We need to make a spiritual investment, which we can do by sharing the spiritual Truths with others. Put another way, we should give love to others.

This should no way encourage anyone to be calculating, but how many seeds of love we sow in good times determines how much help we will get when we face adversity. Whether people offer us help in difficult times will be determined by the love we gave when we were well-off. So in adversity, we should continue strengthening ourselves, and in prosperity, we should sow the seeds of love, or practice love that gives. This sounds like a very simple philosophy, but this is the way to become truly invincible.

When we face hardships, we often ask for what we don't deserve. We despair over our bad luck or misfortune and seek others' help. But when our situation improves, we are apt to become proud of our own achievements and feel as if we succeeded entirely on our own. People leave us when they notice our arrogance. No one wants to help people who become full of themselves in good times but collapse when things get tough.

If you have had an experience in which no one offered you advice until you were faced with serious danger or a crisis, it is probably because you were too proud while things were going well. Those who are full of ego and take others' kindness and praise for granted will have no one to warn them of the danger they are facing. They suddenly find themselves like a clown standing alone in spotlight. All this time, they thought they were popular, but when they pause and look around, they realize that everyone else has left. Facing this harsh reality, they finally ask themselves what it is that they did wrong.

On the other hand, those who constantly care for others and give love in good times no doubt find others willing to offer advice and help when they face a difficulty. Their hearts, filled with love and care for others, offer hope to many, and their acts of love produce virtue. The good they do for others will, without exception, bring in help from others in a time of crisis.

We should always keep this principle in mind, especially if we often find ourselves carried away by our pride or quick to become complacent when success comes easily.

# 11

# SETTING
# A HIGHER GOAL

*There are those who,* having achieved 80 percent of their goal, suddenly lose their way and end up failing. They are like climbers who tumble down the mountain right before they reach the summit. I am sure many people have experienced something going wrong right before they reach their goal. But we need to be able to overcome this tendency if we want to achieve invincible success.

People who succeed to a certain extent but are unable to achieve total success often fear success subconsciously. If they contemplate this pattern deeply, they find that they are scared of achieving their dream. They feel that they don't deserve to realize their dream, so they become nervous as they get closer to it and begin to sow the seeds of their own downfall before they reach their goal. They do something to let success slip through their fingers, or something happens to dash their dreams when they are almost there. The root cause is actually their mind; it is their fear of achieving total success that is preventing them from reaching their dream.

Let's take the example of a couple to illustrate. A wife wishes her husband to be promoted to a higher position so he can earn more. But right before he gets promoted, the wife does something to ruin his reputation, such as spreading a harmful rumor. She does this because she fears becoming a wife of an executive. She is afraid that she won't be good enough for him and that his promotion will eventually destroy their relationship. As a result, she unconsciously does something to stop her husband from getting ahead. This kind of thing happens a lot.

People who fear success do so because they have never experienced real success. That's why they become scared when they see a sign of success ahead. They start worrying that the success will lead to a failure, so they run away from that possibility.

If you find yourself failing right before you reach your goal, you need to make it a habit to set your sights on a higher aim. Whenever you think you are coming close to your initial goal, tell yourself that your current goal is not your final destination, but only a foothold for success. Make a habit of always thinking one step ahead and always having a further goal in sight. Constantly remind yourself that there is always a higher goal that you need to accomplish. If you can do this, you will never find yourself failing. Even if you make mistakes in the short run, you will succeed in the long run.

Developing a habit of setting new goals helps us make a steady progress in life. Some students feel so relieved after an exam that they rush out to let off steam, not caring about the results. This type of person is often destined for failure and feels assailed by life's ups and downs. But those who pull themselves together right after the exam and start preparing for the next one will not easily give in or collapse. So when you think you have achieved your initial goal, focus your mind on your next goal, and start working steadily to achieve it.

# 12

# LEVERAGING DIFFICULTIES
# TO OUR ADVANTAGE

*In judo, we use* leverage to throw our opponent. In the same way, when we practice invincible thinking, instead of focusing exclusively on using our own power to wrestle with our problem, we turn the difficulty or hardship to our advantage and use it to produce something positive. This is the power of invincible thinking.

We may not be able to achieve much with our power alone, but by leveraging external forces to our advantage, we can create something greater. This is an essential attitude we should always keep.

Invincible thinking lets us use the power of leverage, just as in judo, we use our opponent's strength against him. When we are beset by hardships and difficulties, it is not sufficient simply to endure them; we should take advantage of our adversity to score a win. Whenever you face a tough situation, think about how you can use it to your advantage. Ask yourself what the problem that you are now facing is. Once you identify it, work it out and move onto the next problem. By repeating this and making this a habit, you will be able to gradually improve the situation. When we master this art of turning difficulties to our advantage, we will find that the outcome is always positive.

In one of my books, *The Starting Point of Happiness*, I said that we should grow like snowballs, which is basically the same idea as invincible thinking. With this powerful attitude, we focus on expanding ourselves whatever happens. We gain from experiences of success, but at the same time, we turn mistakes and failures into lessons that we can learn from and turn them to our advantage so we can use them as seeds of future success. Living with this perspective makes life more joyful and allows us to keep triumphing throughout our life.

# 13

# LIVING A LIFE OF
# TRIUMPH EVERY DAY

*Invincible thinking and* positive thinking share common ground, but promote different perspectives on life. Positive thinking is based on the idea that all our problems, troubles, and evils essentially do not exist and that only light, which everything is made of, is true existence. Invincible thinking helps us find our purpose in discovering and gaining light from various experiences in this physical world. When we live with this perspective, we find ourselves continually winning in life. In this sense, invincible thinking resembles positive thinking.

The difference between positive thinking and invincible thinking lies in the strength we can cultivate. If we take positive thinking as something that helps us achieve a high level of awareness instantaneously, our growth will be only superficial. But when we grow with invincible thinking, we build the "muscles" of our souls. We turn our day-to-day hardships into inner strength. We may look the same on the outside, but we become much stronger inside.

When we practice invincible thinking, we develop strong, unshakable minds and solid, fortified hearts that are impervious to hardship. With unshakable minds, we can take in problems and troubles just as our white blood cells chase and ingest harmful bacteria one after another, and we can turn those problems into nourishment for the soul. We are prepared for any tribulation and all the vicissitudes of life, because as soon as trouble comes, we absorb it and turn it into our souls' strength. This is a truly empowering attitude that helps us become unshakable under any circumstance.

If good things happen to us, we should be grateful for the help of the many people who made it possible for us to come this far. Think of success not as your accomplishment alone, but as a gift from God that others helped you receive. As the saying goes, "The boughs that bear most hang lowest"—and the more success we reap, the more humble we become. At the same time, the more adversity we face, the stronger we become.

When we cultivate this attitude of taking advantage of difficult times to fertilize our soul and grow, we no longer fear adversity. We are prepared for any hardship and even see hardship as a great opportunity to learn lessons for our improvement. This attitude strengthens us to become new lights that shine upon the world.

In times of setback—when we are demoted, take a pay cut, or go bankrupt—we naturally become introspective. So we should make the most of it by spending time on meditation and contemplation to temper and toughen our soul firmly and thoroughly. If we make constant and constructive efforts, we'll be able to achieve concrete results when things get better.

Put another way, invincible thinking is about taking both Shakyamuni Buddha's self-reflective, introspective attitude and Hermes' constructive, positive attitude*. In the face of adversity, we focus on self-reflection, as taught by Shakyamuni Buddha. In times of success, we aim for further progress and development, as taught by Hermes. At Happy Science, I teach both these ideas, as the principles of self-reflection and progress. Combining these two principles makes us invincible.

Our goal in life should be to keep growing and progressing every year. If we suffer a loss, self-reflection can help us remove the thorn, but we have to get more than that out of it. We shouldn't be complacent with merely weathering a storm until it dies down, only to still be where we started. Instead, we should face the storms that come our way, absorb all we can from our setbacks, and turn them into strength or energy.

When you compare your present self with the way you were one, two, and three years ago, I hope you can see the progress and growth you have made. If you find yourself continually growing like bamboo, you are indeed living a life of triumph every day.

---

* The god Hermes was a hero who lived in Greece 4,300 years ago. He brought prosperity to the Mediterranean region and laid the foundations of Western civilization. Hermes is well-known as the god of commerce, prosperity, the arts, travel, communication, and medicine.

# Afterword

This book, *Invincible Thinking*, offers a philosophy whose principles can guide you to success, abundant life, happiness, and enlightenment. It presents principles and methods of achieving victory in life from a variety of perspectives, interspersed with practical advice throughout the text. As you delve into its pages, you will come to understand that nurturing deep insight into life and cultivating wisdom from our life experiences allow us to build a bridge between self-reflection and spiritual growth.

This book was assembled from a series of four weekday seminars I gave at Happy Science in June and July 1989. It presents the essence of my teachings, and I recommend it as an essential volume for all who seek triumph in this life.

*Ryuho Okawa*

FOUNDER AND CEO
Happy Science Group

# About the Author

RYUHO OKAWA is a global visionary, renowned spiritual leader, and internationally best-selling author with a simple goal: to help people find true happiness and create a better world.

His deep compassion and sense of responsibility for the happiness of each individual has prompted him to publish over 2,200 titles of religious, spiritual, and self-development teachings, covering a broad range of topics including how our thoughts influence reality, the nature of love, and the path to enlightenment. He also writes on the topics of management and economy, as well as the relationship between religion and politics in the global context. To date, Okawa's books have sold over 100 million copies worldwide and been translated into 28 languages.

Okawa has dedicated himself to improving society and creating a better world. In 1986, Okawa founded Happy Science as a spiritual movement dedicated to bringing greater happiness to humankind by uniting religions and cultures to live in harmony. Happy Science has grown rapidly from its beginnings in Japan to a worldwide organization with over twelve million members. Okawa is compassionately committed to the spiritual growth of others. In addition to writing and publishing books, he continues to give lectures around the world.

# About Happy Science

Happy Science is a global movement that empowers individuals to find purpose and spiritual happiness and to share that happiness with their families, societies, and the world. With more than twelve million members around the world, Happy Science aims to increase awareness of spiritual truths and expand our capacity for love, compassion, and joy so that together we can create the kind of world we all wish to live in.

Activities at Happy Science are based on the Principles of Happiness (Love, Wisdom, Self-Reflection, and Progress). These principles embrace worldwide philosophies and beliefs, transcending boundaries of culture and religions.

**Love** teaches us to give ourselves freely without expecting anything in return; it encompasses giving, nurturing, and forgiveness.

**Wisdom** leads us to the insights of spiritual truths, and opens us to the true meaning of life and the will of God (the universe, the highest power, Buddha).

**Self-Reflection** brings a mindful, nonjudgmental lens to our thoughts and actions to help us find our truest selves—the essence of our souls—and deepen our connection to the highest power. It helps us attain a clean and peaceful mind and leads us to the right life path.

**Progress** emphasizes the positive, dynamic aspects of our spiritual growth—actions we can take to manifest and spread happiness around the world. It's a path that not only expands our soul growth, but also furthers the collective potential of the world we live in.

# Programs and Events

The doors of Happy Science are open to all. We offer a variety of programs and events, including self-exploration and self-growth programs, spiritual seminars, meditation and contemplation sessions, study groups, and book events.

For more information, visit happyscience-na.org or happy-science.org.

# International Seminars

Each year, friends from all over the world join our international seminars, held at our faith centers in Japan. Different programs are offered each year and cover a wide variety of topics, including improving relationships, practicing the Eightfold Path to enlightenment, and loving yourself, to name just a few.

# Happy Science Monthly

Our monthly publication covers the latest featured lectures, members' life-changing experiences and other news from members around the world, book reviews, and many other topics. Downloadable PDF files are available at happyscience-na.org. Copies and back issues in Portuguese, Chinese, and other languages are available upon request. For more information, contact us via e-mail at tokyo@happy-science.org.

# Contact Information

Happy Science is a worldwide organization with faith centers around the globe. For a comprehensive list of centers, visit the worldwide directory at happy-science.org or happyscience-na.org. The following are some of the many Happy Science locations:

## United States and Canada

**NEW YORK**
79 Franklin Street
New York, NY 10013
Phone: 212-343-7972
Fax: 212-343-7973
Email: ny@happy-science.org
Website: newyork.happyscience-na.org

**NEW JERSEY**
725 River Rd. #102B
Edgewater, NJ 07020
Phone: 201-313-0127
Fax: 201-313-0120
Email: nj@happy-science.org
Website: newjersey.happyscience-na.org

**FLORIDA**
5208 8th St.
Zephyrhills, FL 33542
Phone: 813-715-0000
Fax: 813-715-0010
Email: florida@happy-science.org
Website: florida.happyscience-na.org

**ATLANTA**
1874 Piedmont Ave. NE
Suite 360-C
Atlanta, GA 30324
Phone: 404-892-7770
Email: atlanta@happy-science.org
Website: atlanta.happyscience-na.org

**SAN FRANCISCO**
525 Clinton Street
Redwood City, CA 94062
Phone&Fax: 650-363-2777
Email: sf@happy-science.org
Website: sanfrancisco.happyscience-na.org

**LOS ANGELES**
1590 E. Del Mar Blvd.
Pasadena, CA 91106
Phone: 626-395-7775
Fax: 626-395-7776
Email: la@happy-science.org
Website: losangeles.happyscience-na.org

**ORANGE COUNTY**
10231 Slater Ave #204
Fountain Valley, CA 92708
Phone: 714-745-1140
Email: oc@happy-science.org

**SAN DIEGO**
7841 Balboa Ave. Suite #202
San Diego, CA 92111
Phone: 619-381-7615
Fax: 626-395-7776
E-mail: sandiego@happy-science.org
Website: happyscience-la.org

**HAWAII**
1221 Kapiolani Blvd. Suite 920
Honolulu, HI 96814
Phone: 808-591-9772
Fax: 808-591-9776
Email: hi@happy-science.org
Website: hawaii.happyscience-na.org

**KAUAI**
4504 Kukui Street
Dragon Building Suite 21
Kapaa, HI 96746
Phone: 808-822-7007
Fax: 808-822-6007
Email: kauai-hi@happy-science.org
Website: kauai.happyscience-na.org

**TORONTO**
845 The Queensway Etobicoke,
ON M8Z 1N6 Canada
Toronto, ON M5T 1S2 Canada
Phone: 1-416-901-3747
Email: toronto@happy-science.org
Website: happy-science.ca

**VANCOUVER**
#212-2609 East 49th Avenue
Vancouver, BC,V5S 1J9 Canada
Phone: 1-604-437-7735
Fax: 1-604-437-7764
Email: vancouver@happy-science.org
Website: happy-science.ca

# International

**TOKYO**
1-6-7 Togoshi, Shinagawa
Tokyo, 142-0041 Japan
Phone: 81-3-6384-5770
Fax: 81-3-6384-5776
Email: tokyo@happy-science.org
Website: happy-science.org

**LONDON**
3 Margaret Street
London, W1W 8RE
United Kingdom
Phone: 44-20-7323-9255
Fax: 44-20-7323-9344
Email: eu@happy-science.org
Website: happyscience-uk.org

**SYDNEY**
516 Pacific Hwy Lane Cove North,
NSW 2066 Australia
Phone: 61-2-9411-2877
Fax: 61-2-9411-2822
Email: sydney@happy-science.org

## BRAZIL HEADQUARTERS

Rua. Domingos de Morais 1154,
Vila Mariana, Sao Paulo,
SP-CEP 04009-002 Brazil
Phone: 55-11-5088-3800
Fax: 55-11-5088-3806
Email: sp@happy-science.org
Website: cienciadafelicidade.com.br

## JUNDIAI

Rua Congo, 447, Jd. Bonfiglioli
Jundiai-CEP 13207-340 Brazil
Phone: 55-11-4587-5952
Email: jundiai@happy-sciece.org

## SEOUL

74, Sadang-ro 27-gil,
Dongjak-gu, Seoul, Korea
Phone: 82-2-3478-8777
Fax: 82-2- 3478-9777
Email: korea@happy-science.org
Website: happyscience-korea.org

## TAIPEI

No. 89, Lane 155,
Dunhua N. Road Songshan District,
Taipei City, 105 Taiwan
Phone: 886-2-2719-9377
Fax: 886-2-2719-5570
Email: taiwan@happy-science.org
Website: happyscience-tw.org

## MALAYSIA

No 22A, Block2, Jalil Link Jalan Jalil
Jaya 2, Bukit Jalil 57000
Kuala Lumpur, Malaysia
Phone: 60-3-8998-7877
Fax: 60-3-8998-7977
Email: malaysia@happy-science.org
Website: happyscience.org.my

## NEPAL

Kathmandu Metropolitan City
Ward No. 15, Ring Road, Kimdol,
Sitapaila Kathmandu, Nepal
Phone: 97-714-272931
Email: nepal@happy-science.org

## UGANDA

Plot 877 Rubaga Road
Kampala P.O. Box 34130
Kampala, Uganda
Phone: 256-79-3238-002
Email: uganda@happy-science.org
Website: happyscience-uganda.org

# About
# IRH Press USA

IRH Press USA Inc. was founded in 2013 as an affiliated firm of IRH Press Co., Ltd. Based in New York, the press publishes books in various categories including spirituality, religion, and self-improvement and publishes books by Ryuho Okawa, the author of 100 million books sold worldwide. For more information, visit OkawaBooks.com.

FOLLOW US ON:

**Facebook:** Okawa Books
**Twitter:** Okawa Books
**Goodreads:** Ryuho Okawa
**Instagram:** OkawaBooks
**Pinterest:** Okawa Books

# Books by Ryuho Okawa

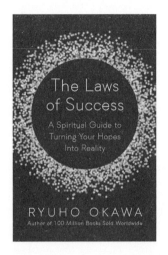

## THE LAWS OF SUCCESS
A Spiritual Guide to Turning Your Hopes Into Reality

Softcover | 208 pages | $15.95 | ISBN: 978-1-942125-15-0

*The Laws of Success* is the modern world's universal guide to happiness and success in all aspects of life. You will find timeless wisdom, the secrets of living with purpose, and practical steps you can take to bring joy and fulfilment to your work and to the lives of others. Ryuho Okawa offers key mindsets, attitudes, and principles that will empower you to make your hopes and dreams come true, inspire you to triumph over setbacks and despair, and help you live every day positively, constructively, and meaningfully.

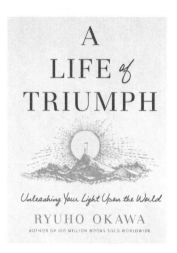

## A LIFE OF TRIUMPH
### Unleashing Your Light Upon the World

Softcover | 240 pages | $15.95 | ISBN: 978-1-942125-11-2

There is a power within you that can lift your heart from despair to hope, from hardship to happiness, and from defeat to triumph. In this book, Ryuho Okawa explains the key attitudes that will help you continuously tap the everlasting reserves of positivity, courage, and energy that are already a part of you so you can realize your dreams and become a wellspring of happiness. You'll also find many inspirational poems and a contemplation exercise to inspirit your inner light in times of adversity and in your day-to-day life.

# HEALING FROM WITHIN
Life-Changing Keys to Calm, Spiritual, and Healthy Living

# THE UNHAPPINESS SYNDROME
28 Habits of Unhappy People (and How to Change Them)

# THE MIRACLE OF MEDITATION
Opening Your Life to Peace, Joy, and the Power Within

# THE ESSENCE OF BUDDHA
The Path to Enlightenment

# THE LAWS OF JUSTICE
How We Can Solve World Conflicts and Bring Peace

# THE HEART OF WORK
10 Keys to Living Your Calling

# THINK BIG!
Be Positive and Be Brave to Achieve Your Dreams

# INVITATION TO HAPPINESS
7 Inspirations from Your Inner Angel

# MESSAGES FROM HEAVEN
What Jesus, Buddha, Muhammad,
and Moses Would Say Today

# THE LAWS OF THE SUN
One Source, One Planet, One People

# SECRETS OF
# THE EVERLASTING TRUTHS
A New Paradigm for Living on Earth

# THE NINE DIMENSIONS
Unveiling the Laws of Eternity

# THE MOMENT OF TRUTH
Become a Living Angel Today

# CHANGE YOUR LIFE,
# CHANGE THE WORLD
A Spiritual Guide to Living Now

*For a complete list of books, visit OkawaBooks.com.*